PLEASE READ THE FOLLOWING BEFORE YOUR HUNTING ADVENTURE

1 NO REAL GUNS NEEDED

All you need is a pen or pencil. A pencil is encouraged if you plan to play more then one time.

2 WILL BE REQUIRED TO CLOSE EYES

this game requires you to close your eyes while "shooting",don't play while driving or operating machinery

3 THIS GAME CAN BECOME ADDICTING

Make sure to take breaks, hunting can be strenuou.

4 STAY FOCUSED

The key to this game is to be focused.

REMEMBER SAFETY FIRST

HOW TO PLAY

All you need is a pen or pencil. A pencil is encouraged if you plan to play more then one time.

1 FOCUS ON TARGET FOR 5 SECONDS WITH EYES OPEN

2 NOW CLOSE YOUR EYES AND WITH YOUR PENCIL OR PEN MAKE A MARK ON THE TARGET WHERE YOU LAST REMEMBER SEEING THE SPOT YOU WERE AIMING FOR. REMEMBER TO KEEP EYES CLOSED FOR EVERY SHOT.

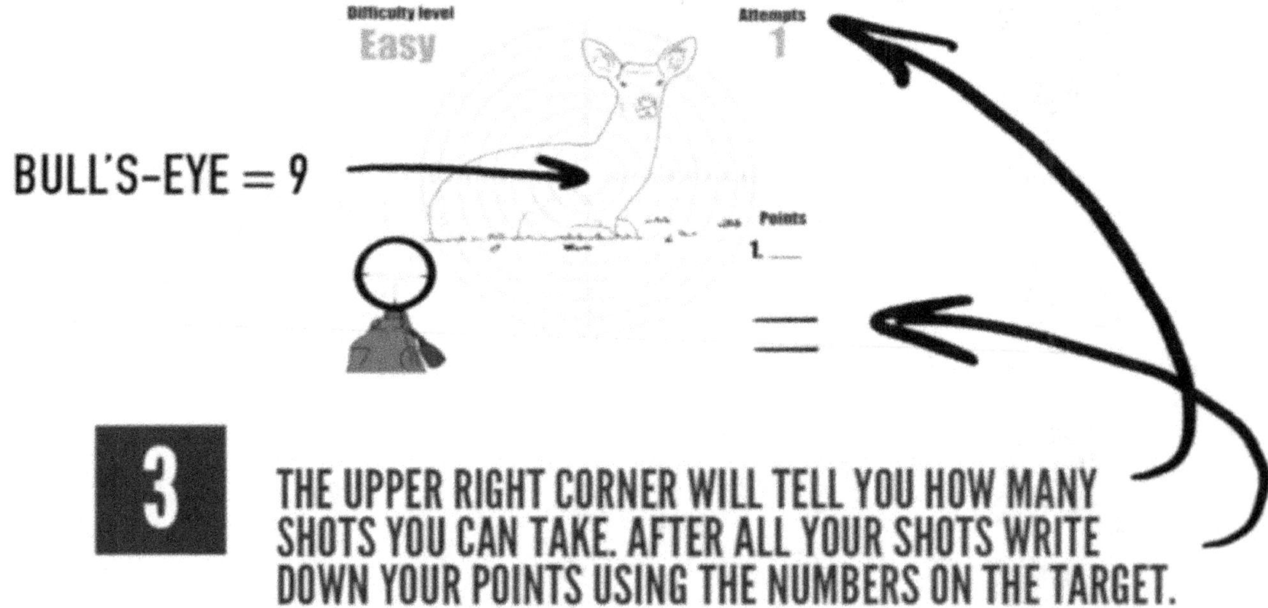

3 THE UPPER RIGHT CORNER WILL TELL YOU HOW MANY SHOTS YOU CAN TAKE. AFTER ALL YOUR SHOTS WRITE DOWN YOUR POINTS USING THE NUMBERS ON THE TARGET.

THATS IT, YOU'RE READY TO HUNT!

Difficulty level

Easy

Attempts

1

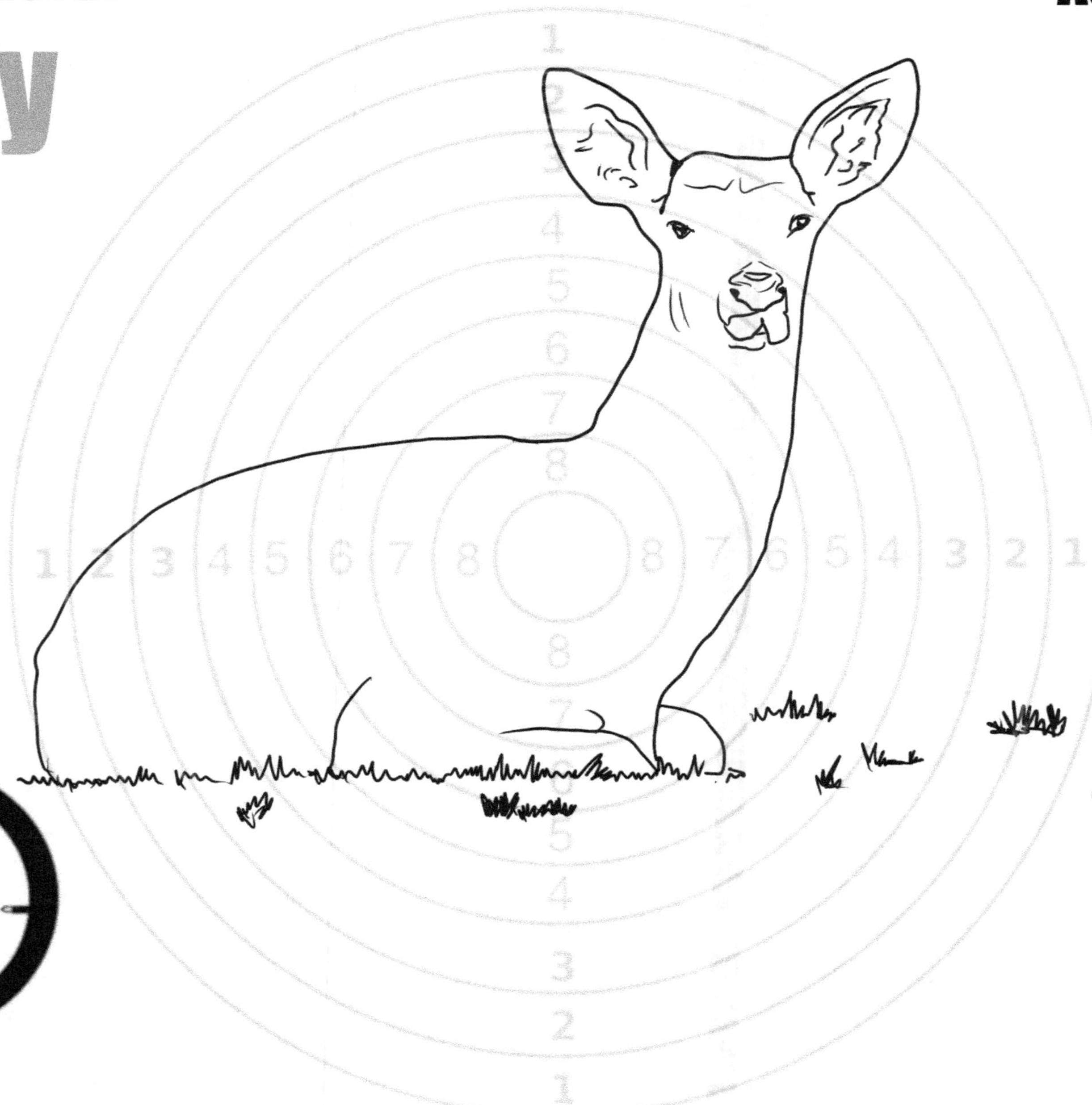

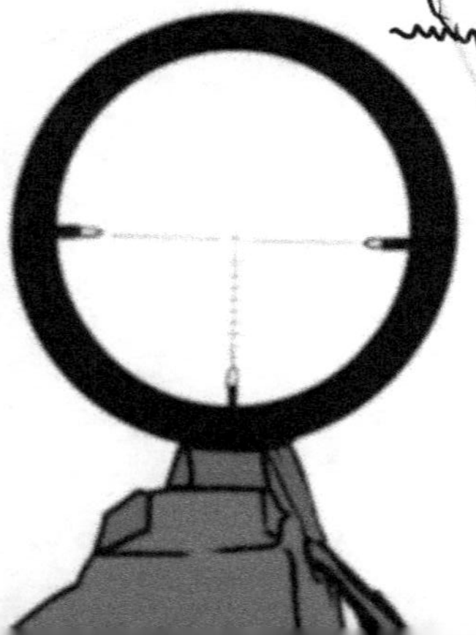

Points

1. ___

___

Difficulty level

Easy

Attempts

1

Points

1. _____

____

Points

1. ___

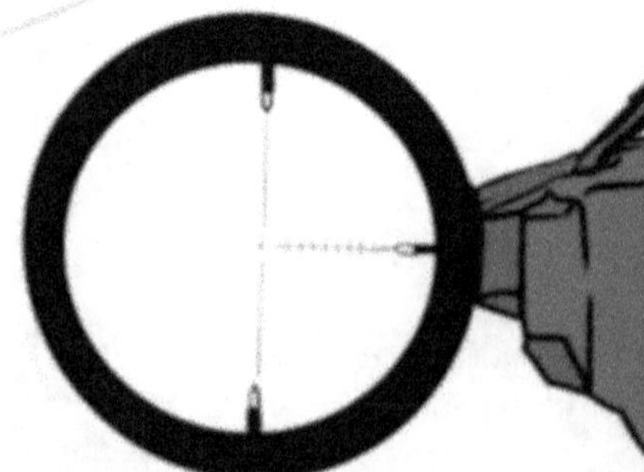

Medium

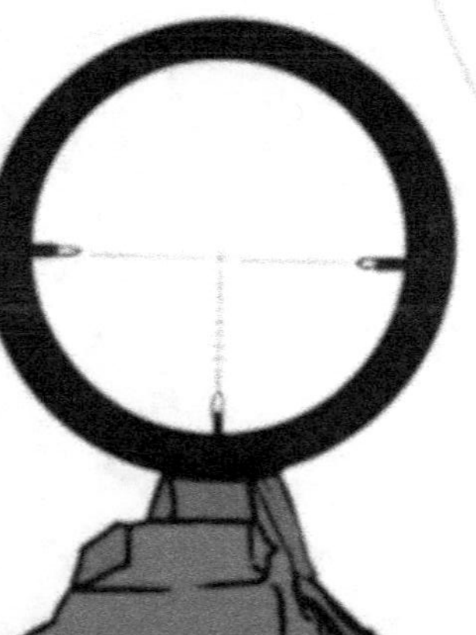

Points

1. ___

2. ___

Difficulty level
Easy
Attempts
1 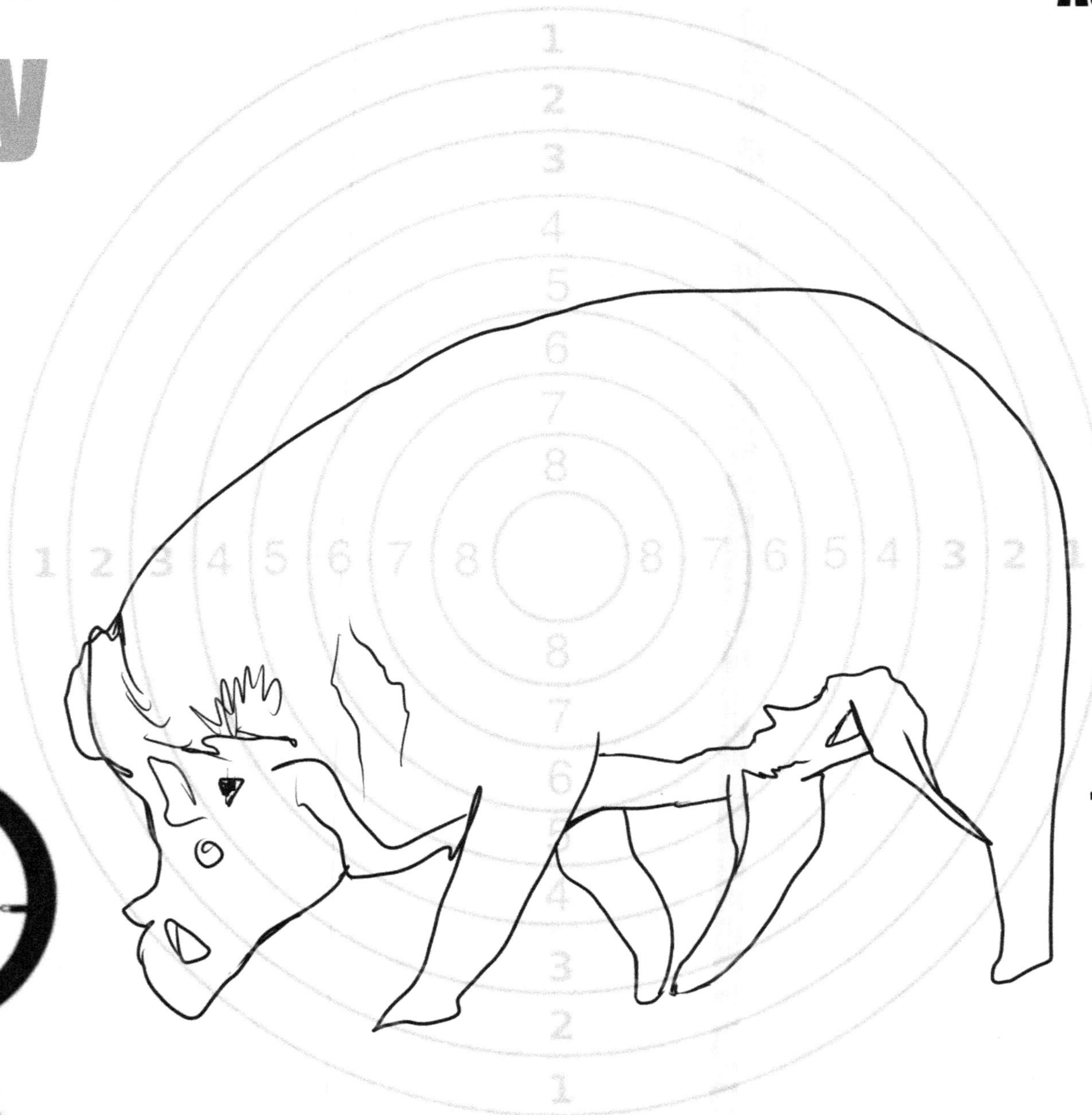 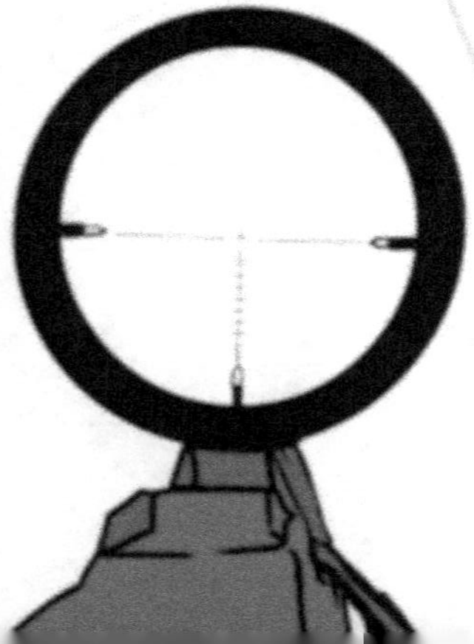
Points
1. ___

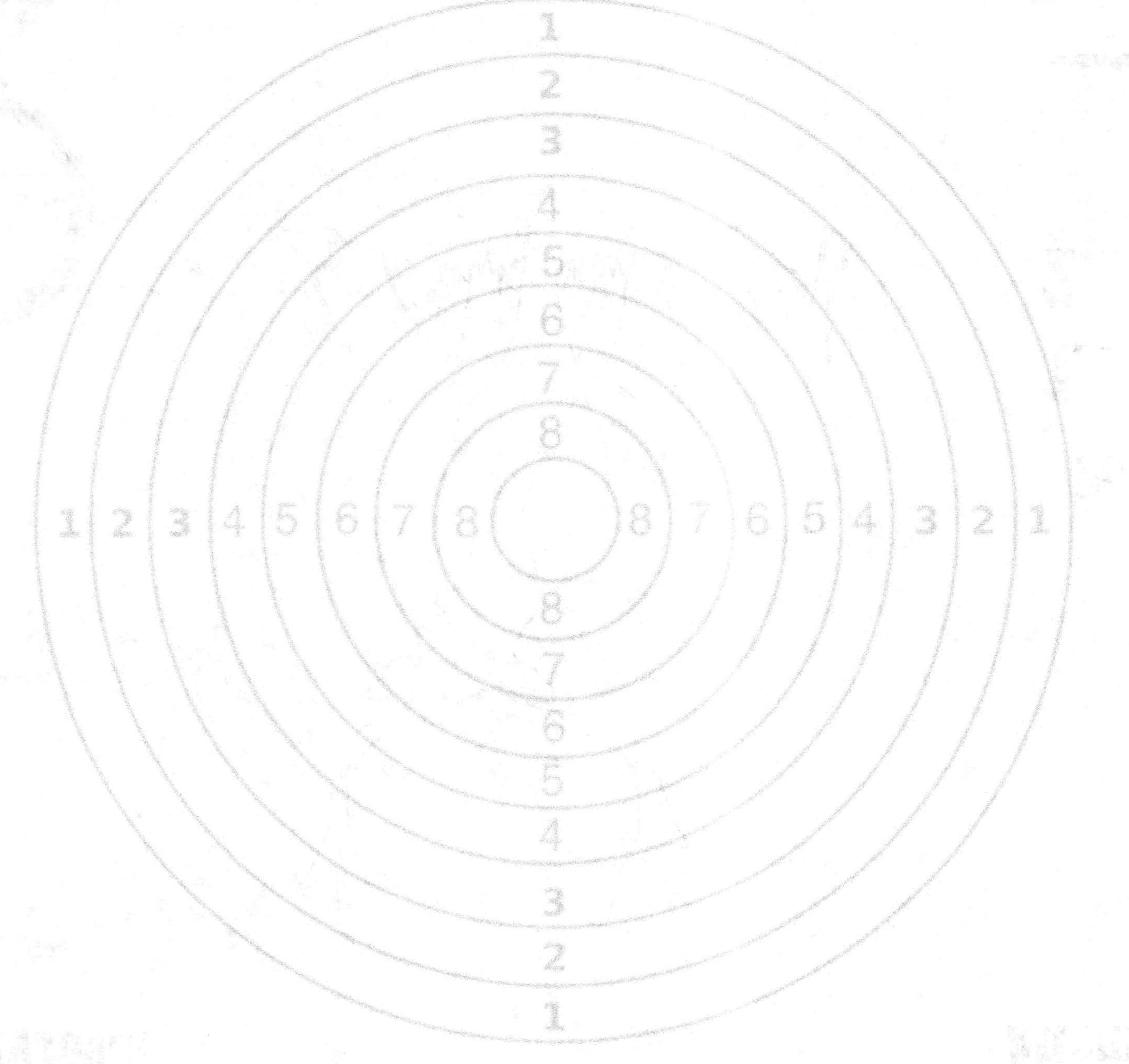

1 2 3 4 5 6 7 8 8 7 6 5 4 3 2 1
1 2 3 4 5 6 7 8 8 7 6 5 4 3 2 1

Difficulty level
Medium

Attempts

2

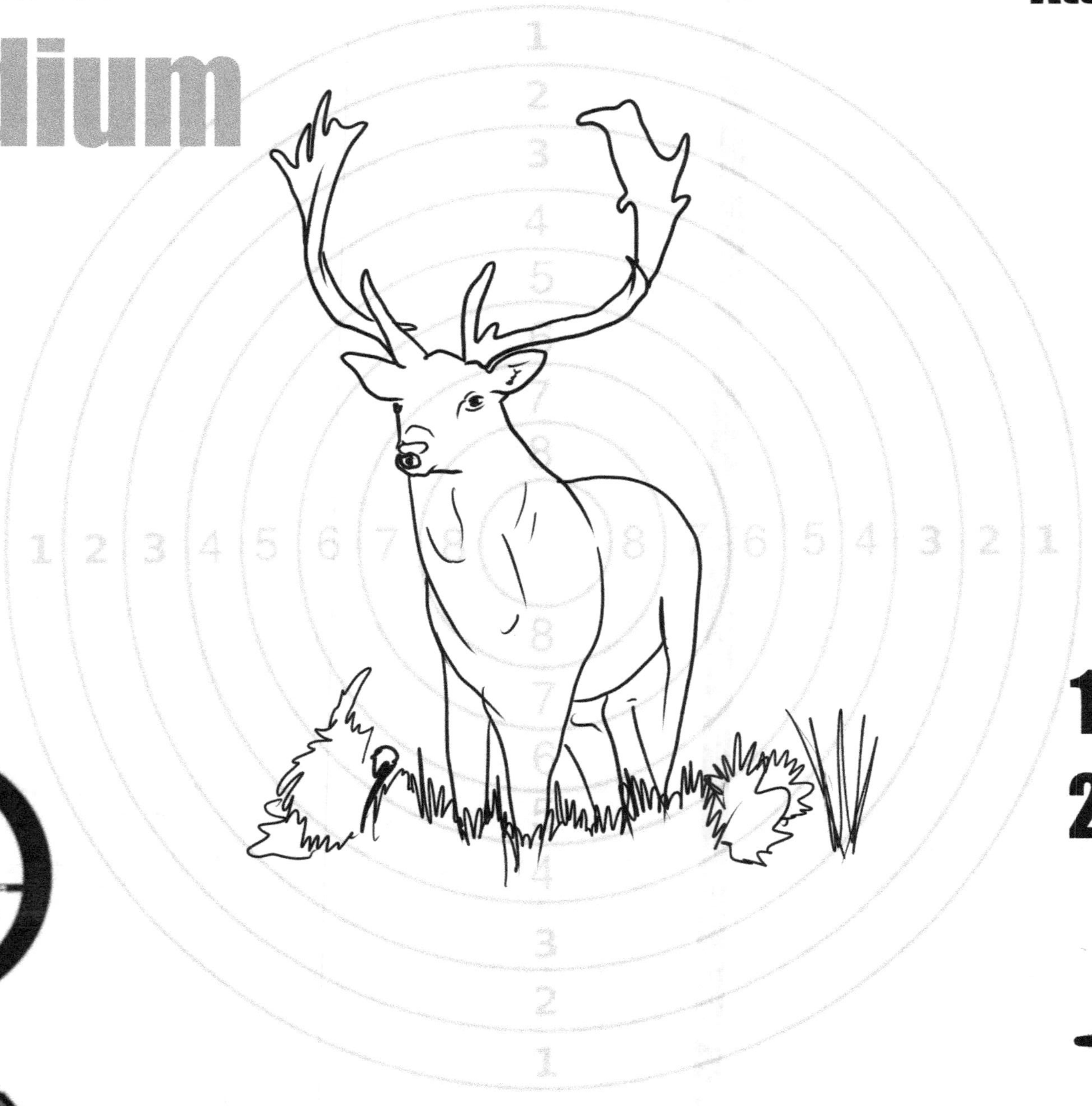

Points

1. ____

2. ____

____

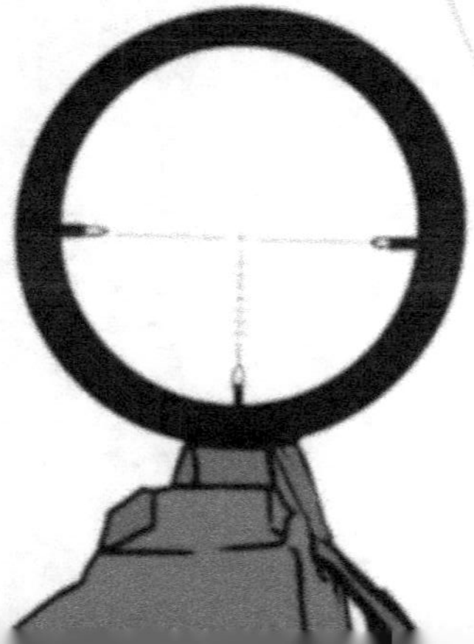

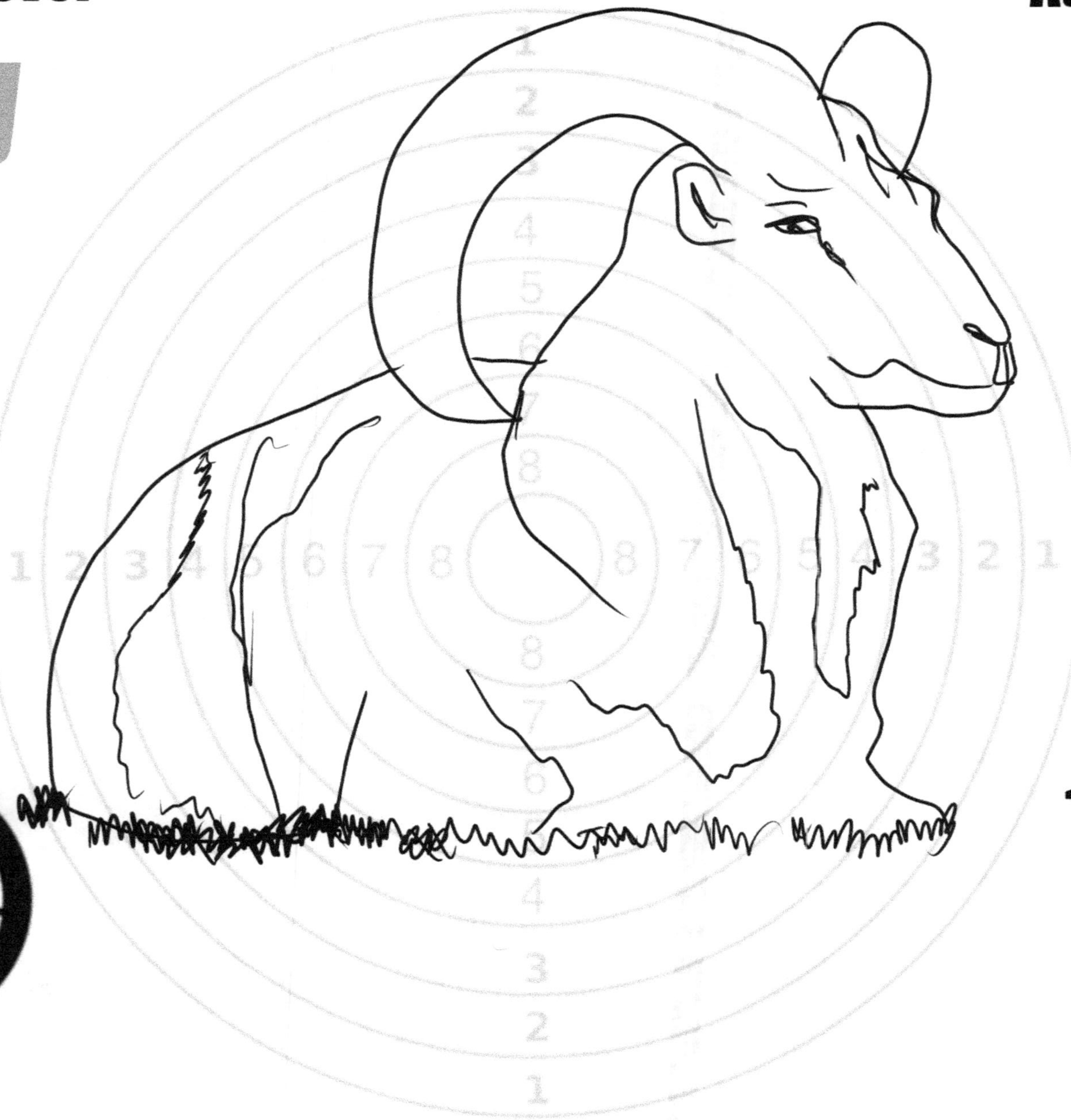

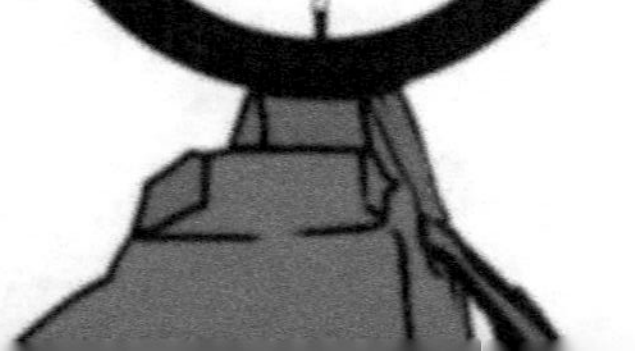

Points

1. ___

Difficulty level
Medium

Attempts
2

Points

1. ____

2. ____

____

Difficulty level
Medium
Attempts
2 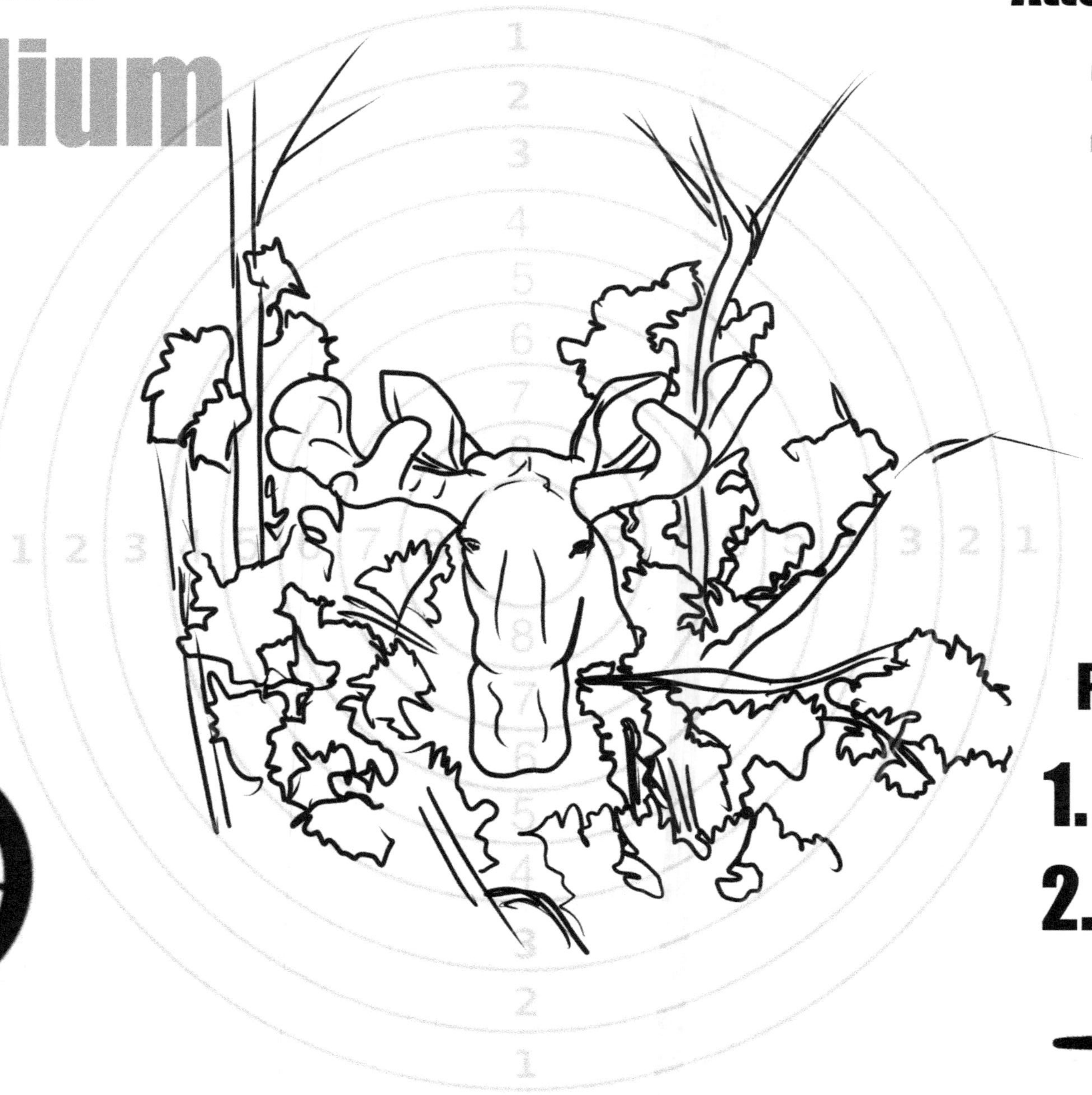 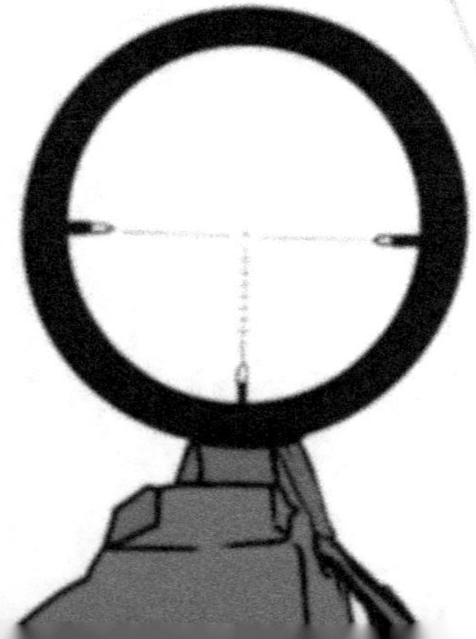
Points
1.
2.

Difficulty level

Easy

Attempts

1

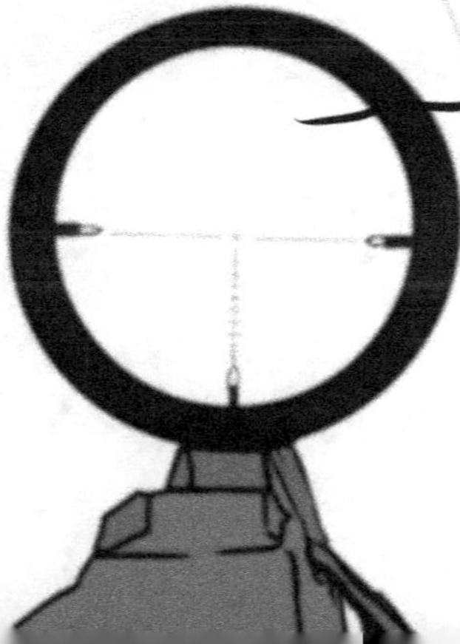

Points

1. _______

1 2 3 4 5 6 7 8 8 7 6 5 4 3 2 1
1
2
3
4
5
6
7
8
8
7
6
5
4
3
2
1

Difficulty level

Hard

Attempts

3

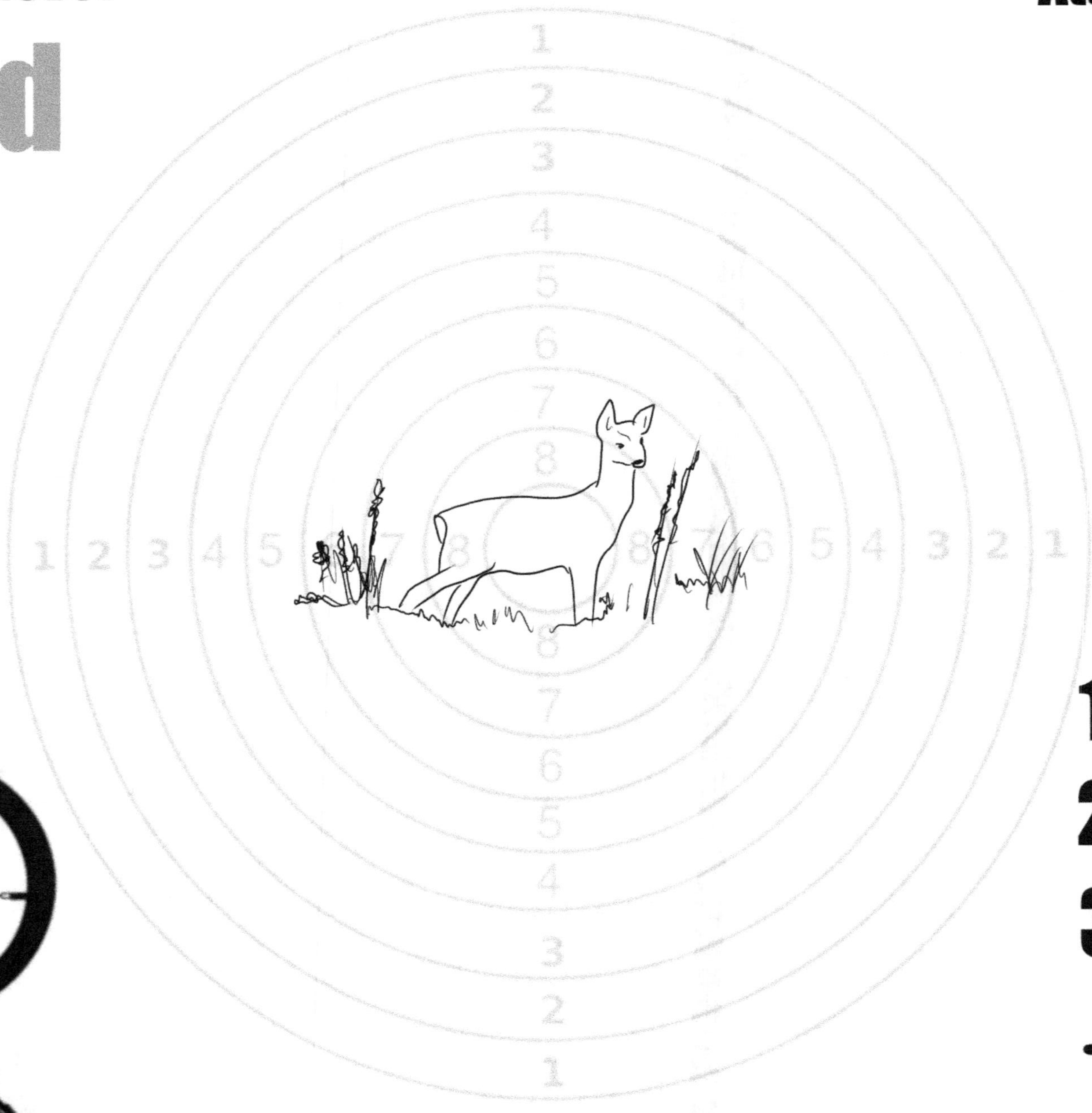

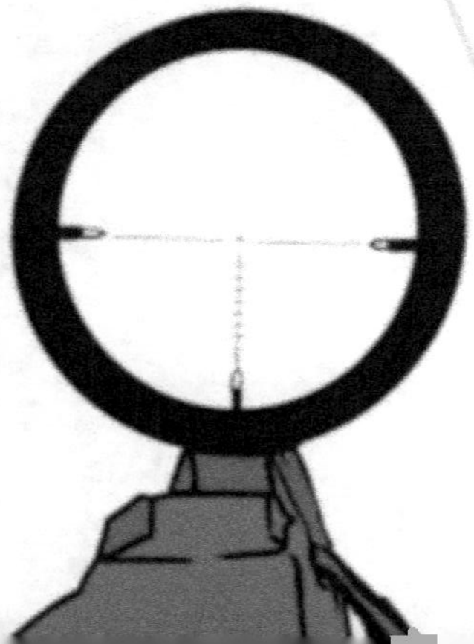

Points

1. ____

2. ____

3. ____

____

Difficulty level
Medium
Attempts
2 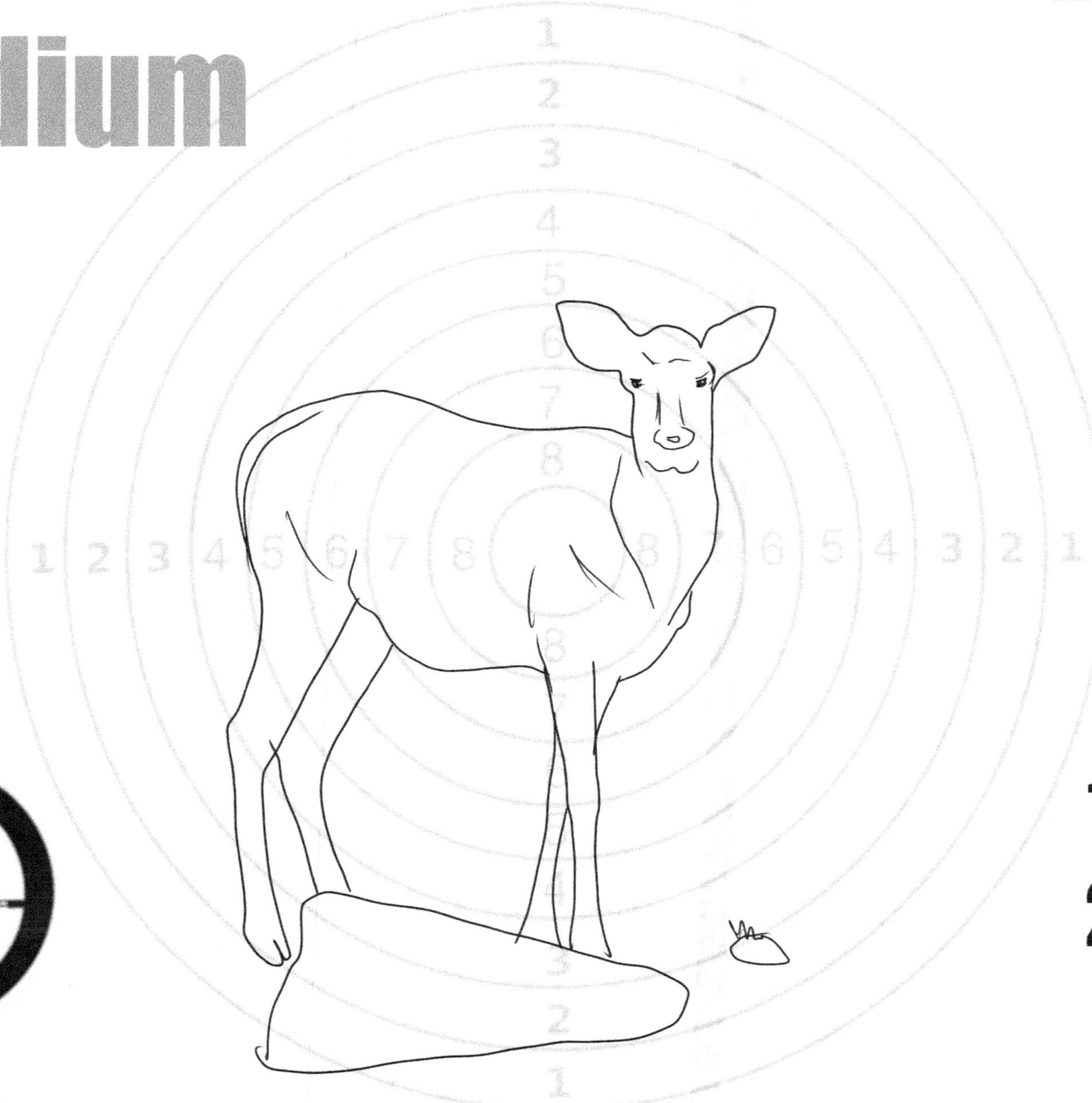 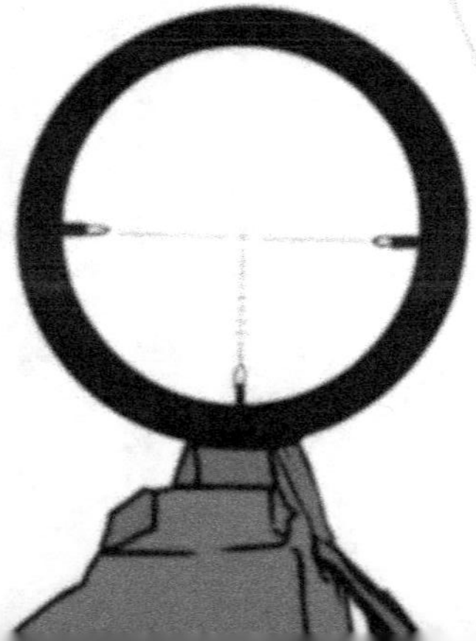
Points
1.
2.

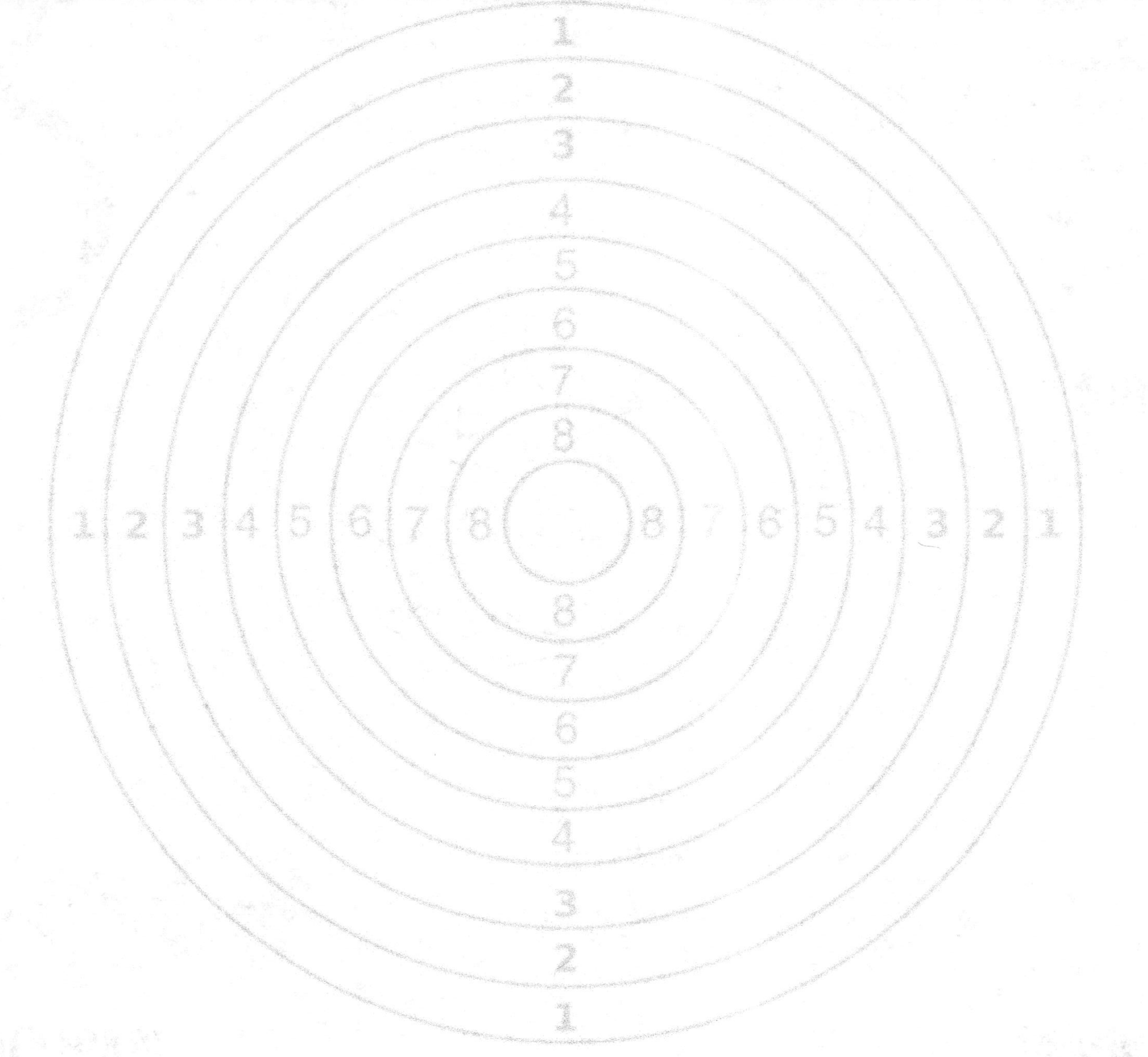

1 2 3 4 5 6 7 8 8 7 6 5 4 3 2 1
1 2 3 4 5 6 7 8 8 7 6 5 4 3 2 1

Difficulty level
Medium
Attempts
2 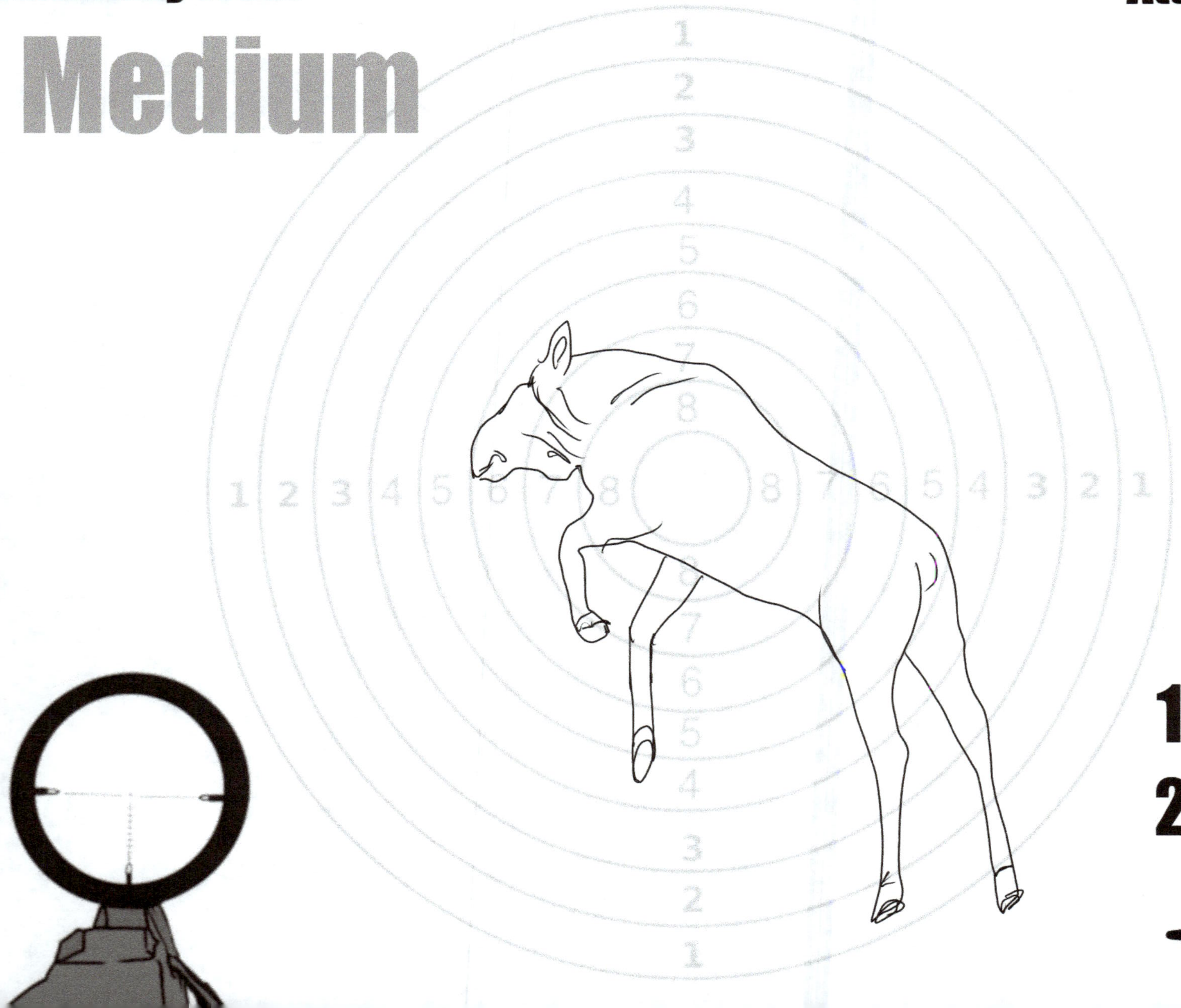
Points
1. ____
2. ____

Points

1. ____
2. ____

____

Difficulty level

Easy

Attempts

1

Points

1. ___

___

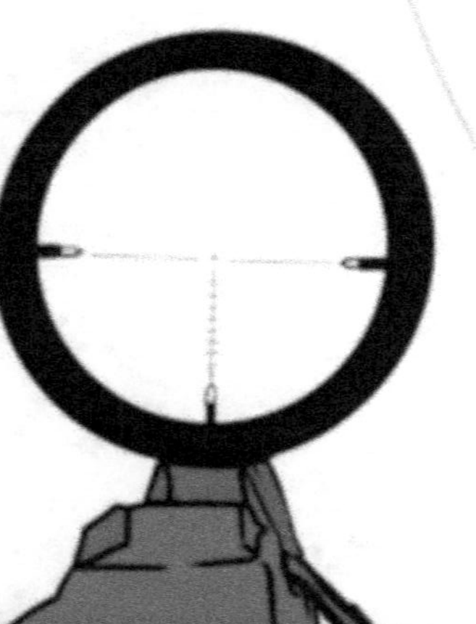

Difficulty level
Medium
Attempts
2 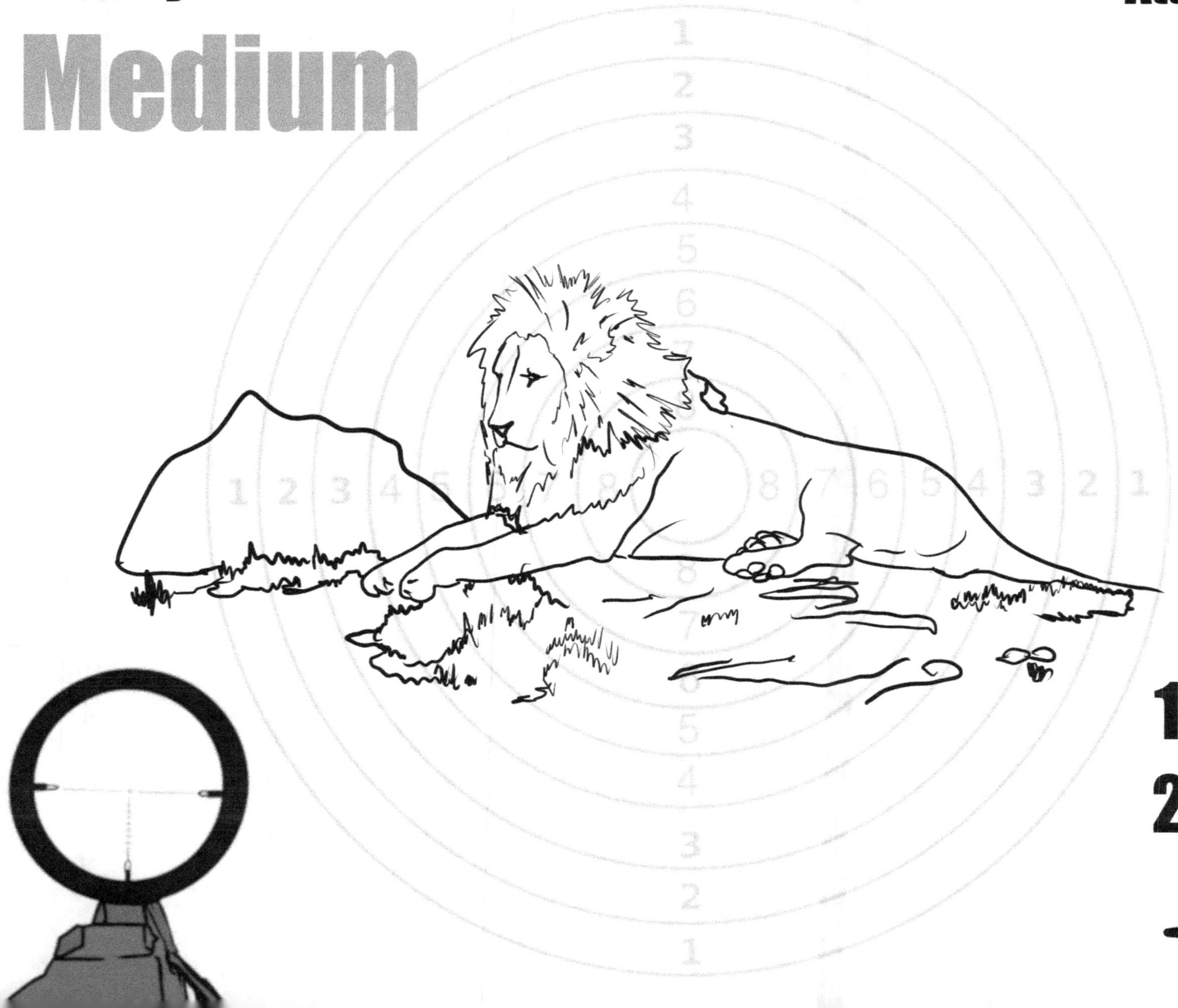
Points
1.
2.

Difficulty level
Medium

Attempts
2

Points

1. ____

2. ____

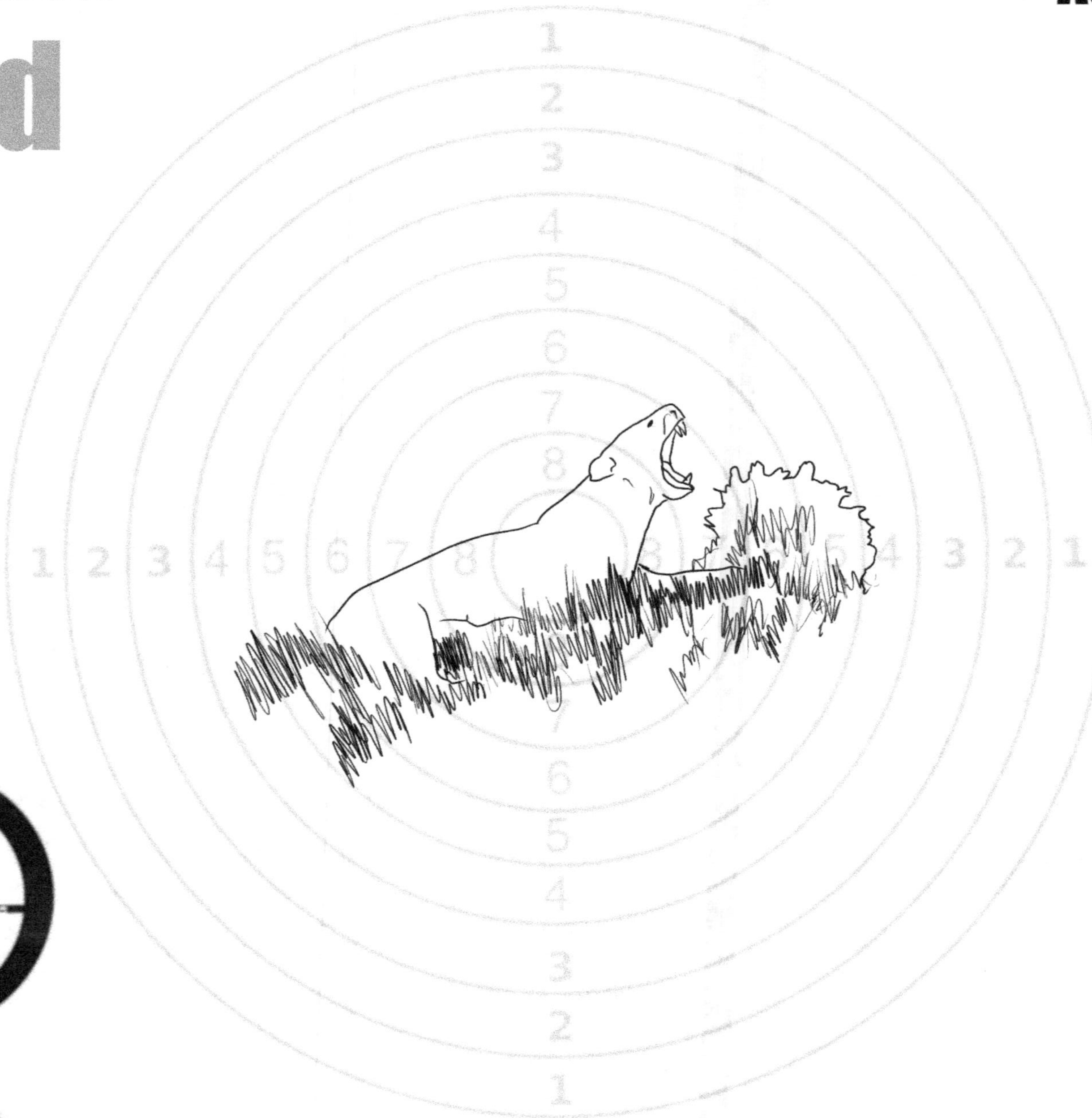

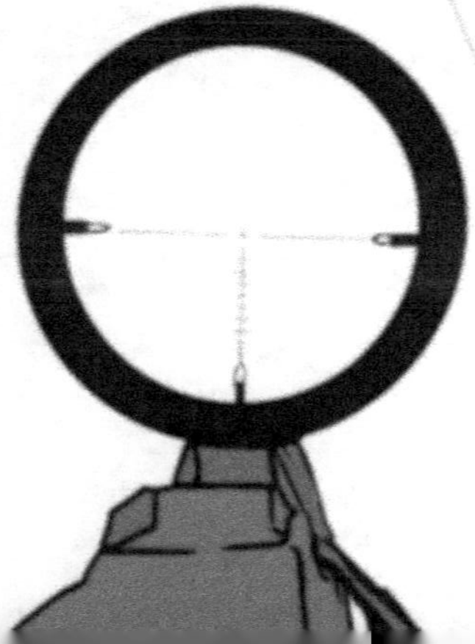

Points

1. ____

2. ____

3. ____

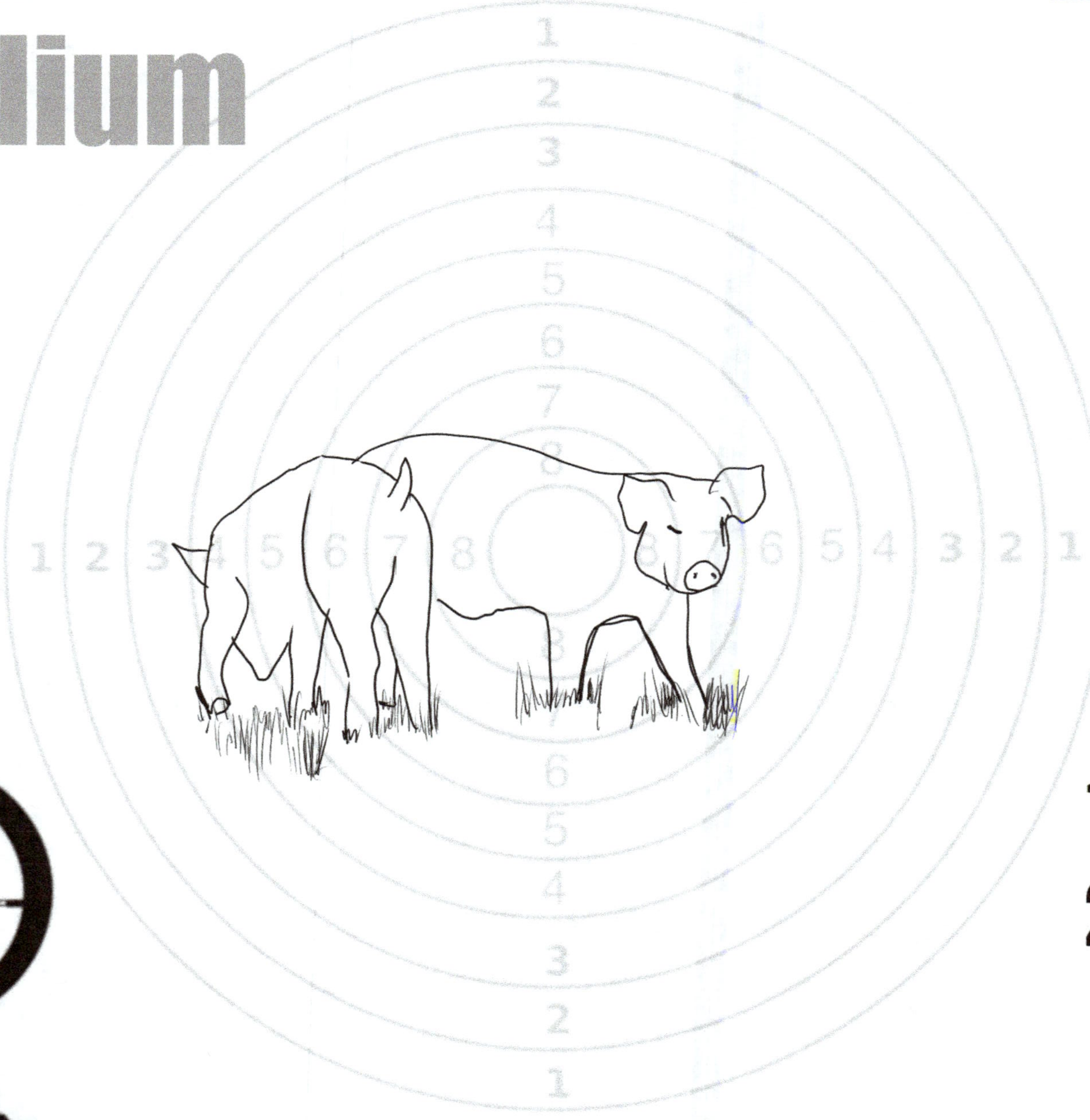

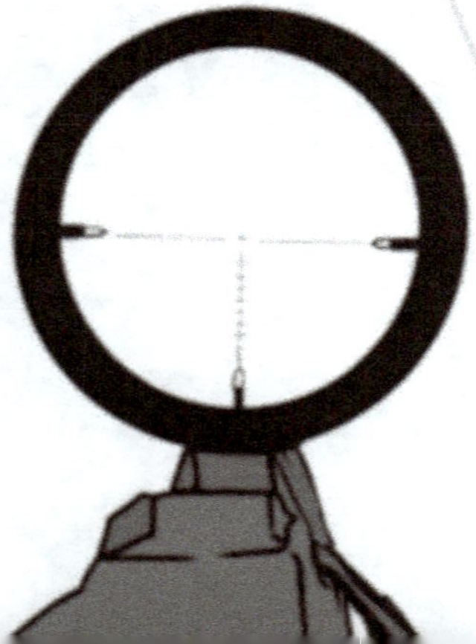

Points

1. ____
2. ____

____

Points

1. _____

____

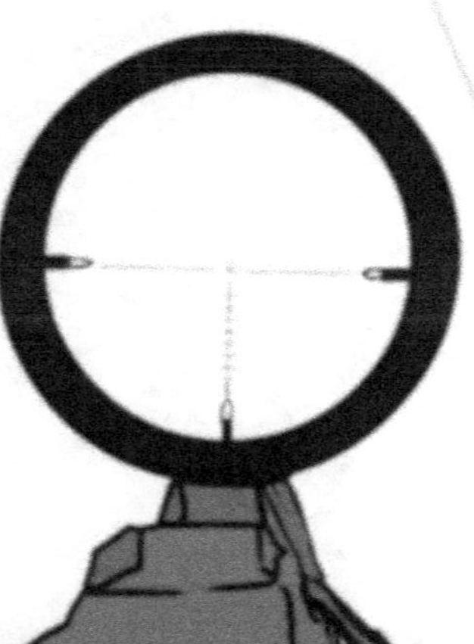

Difficulty level
Easy
Attempts
1  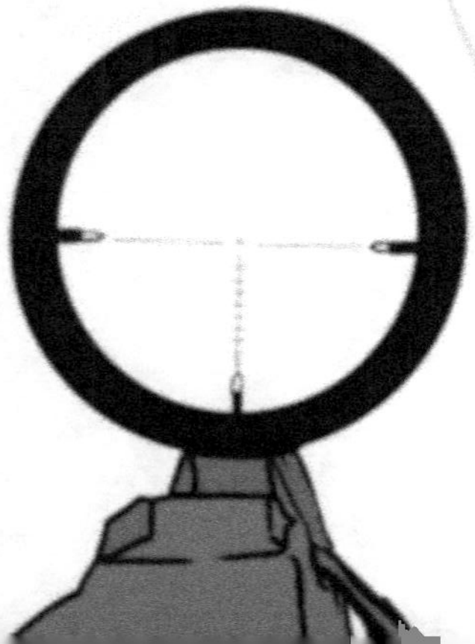
Points
1. ____

Difficulty level

Easy

Attempts

1

Points

1. ___

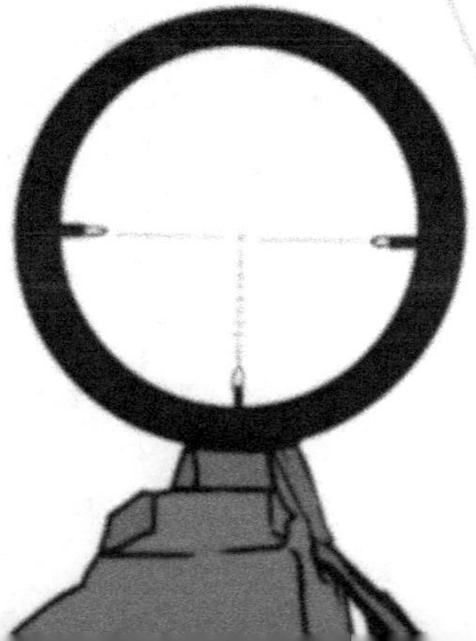

___

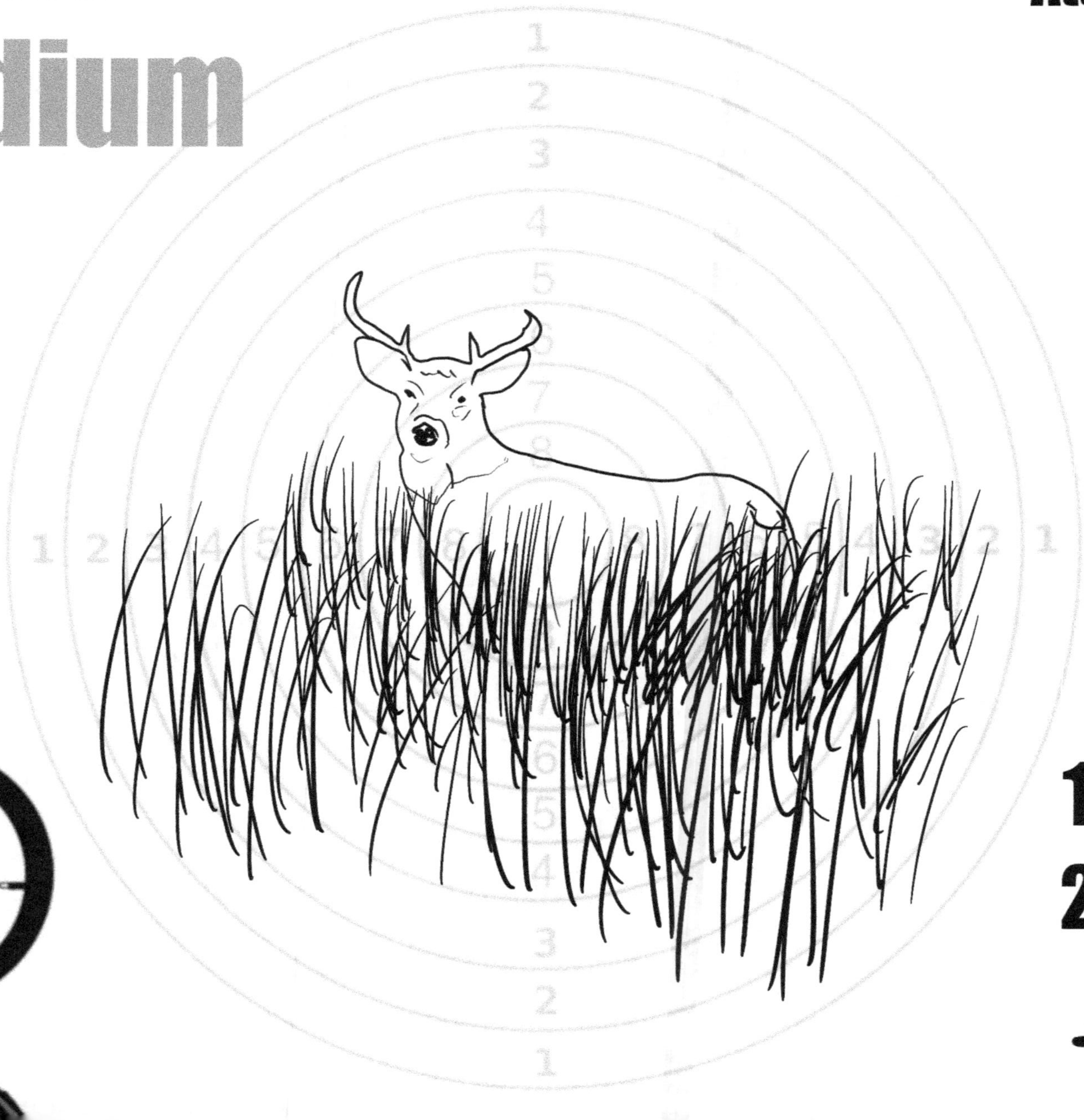

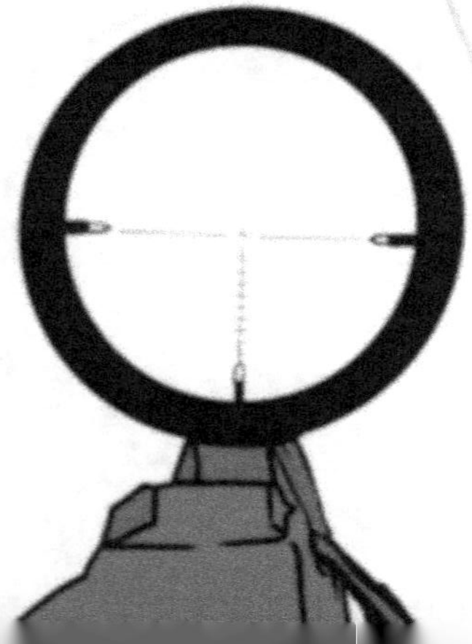

Points

1. ___

2. ___

___

Difficulty level

Hard

Attempts

3

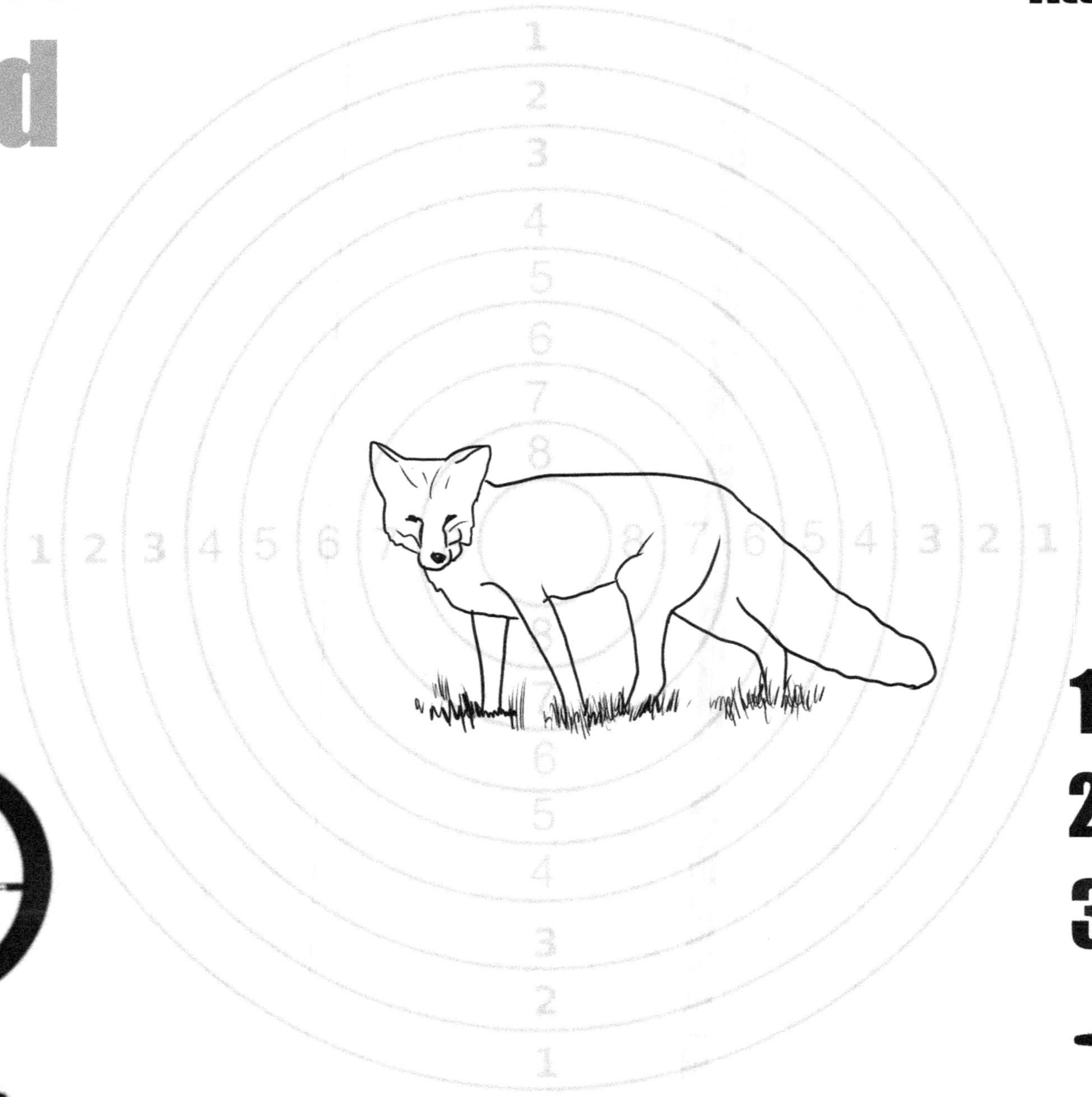

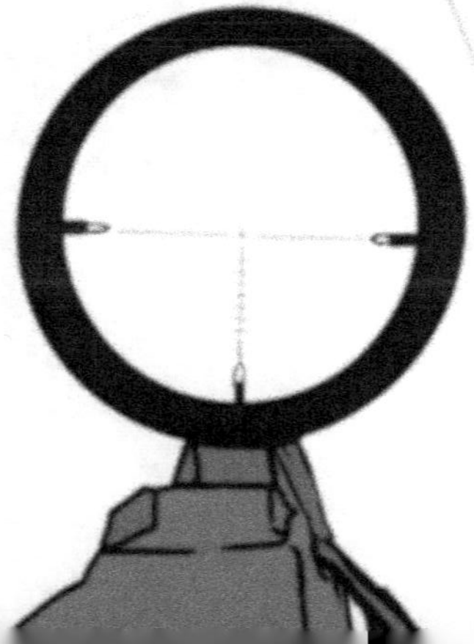

Points

1. ____

2. ____

3. ____

____

Difficulty level
Hard
Attempts
3 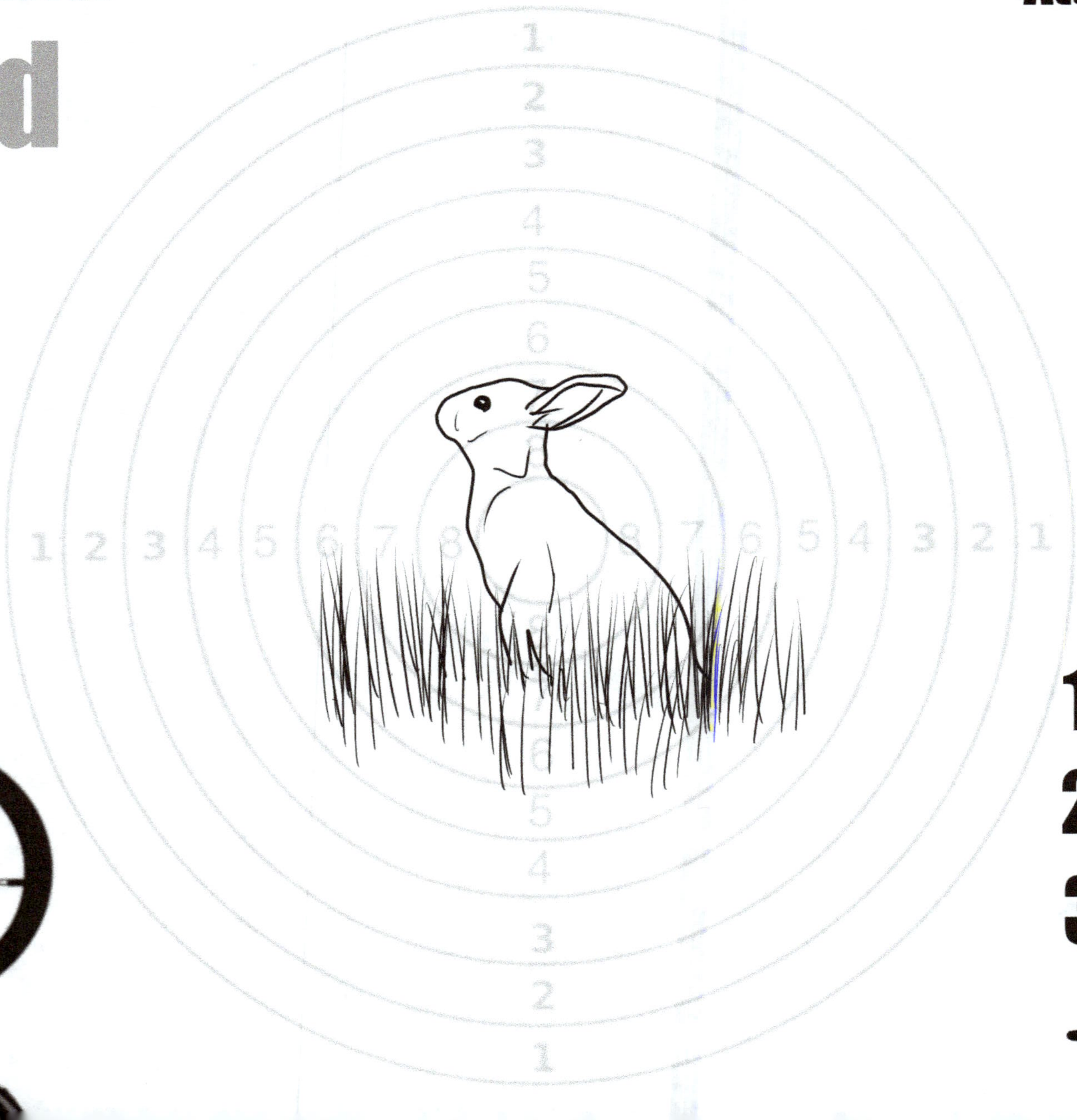 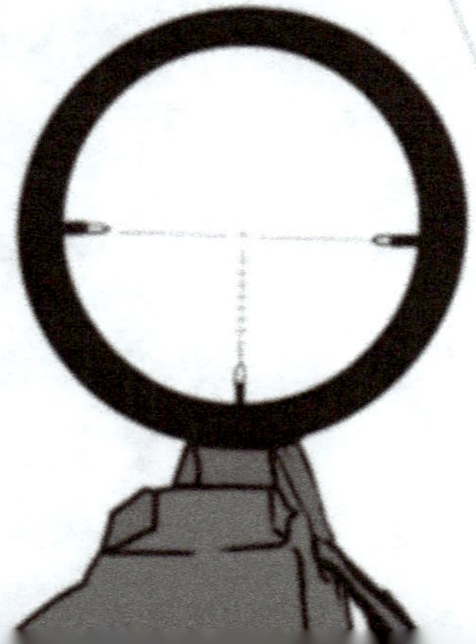
Points
1. ___
2. ___
3. ___
___

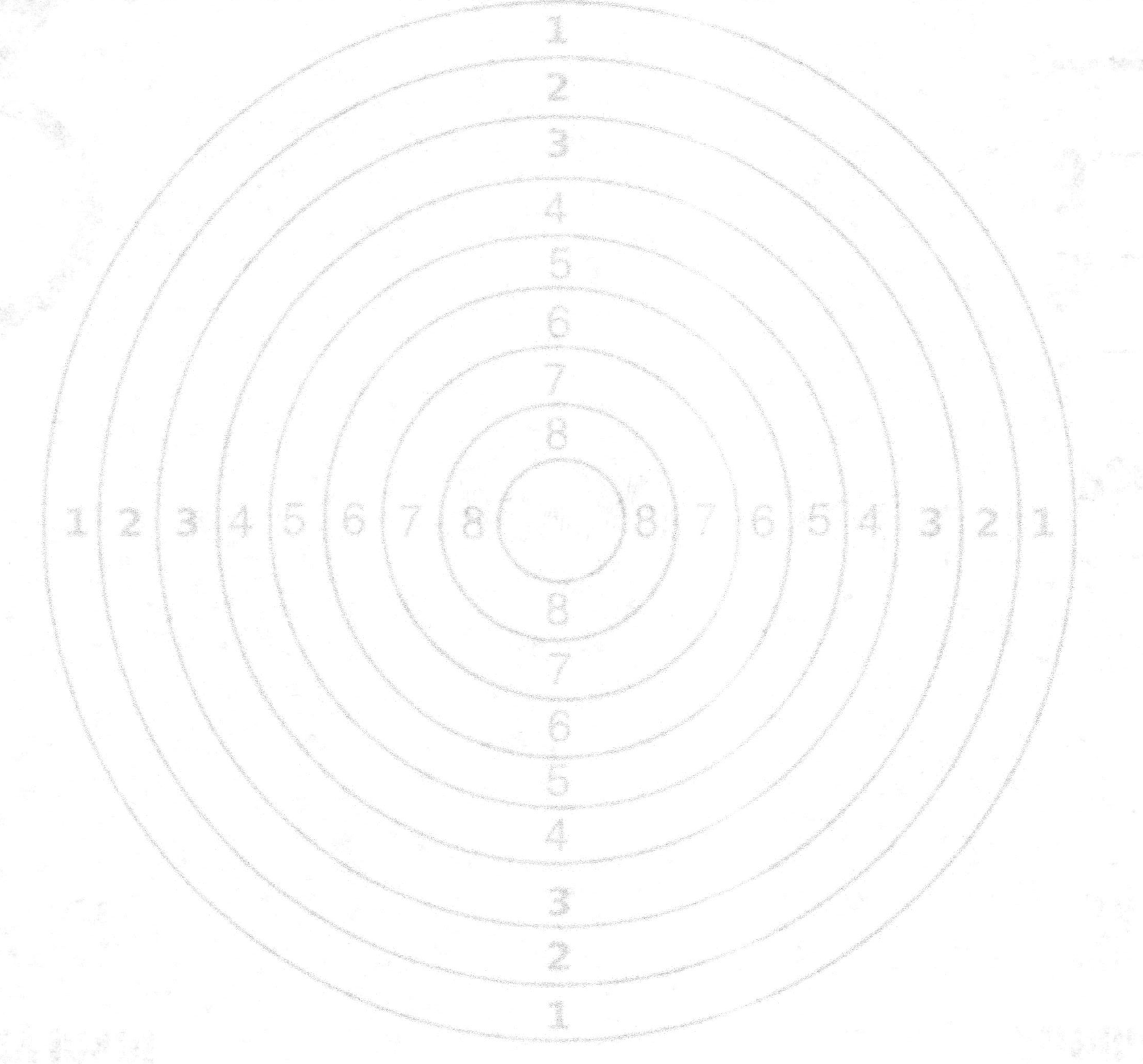

1
2
3
4
5
6
7
8
1 2 3 4 5 6 7 8 8 7 6 5 4 3 2 1
8
7
6
5
4
3
2
1

Difficulty level

Hard

Attempts

3

Points

1. ___

2. ___

3. ___

___

Difficulty level

Hard

Attempts

3

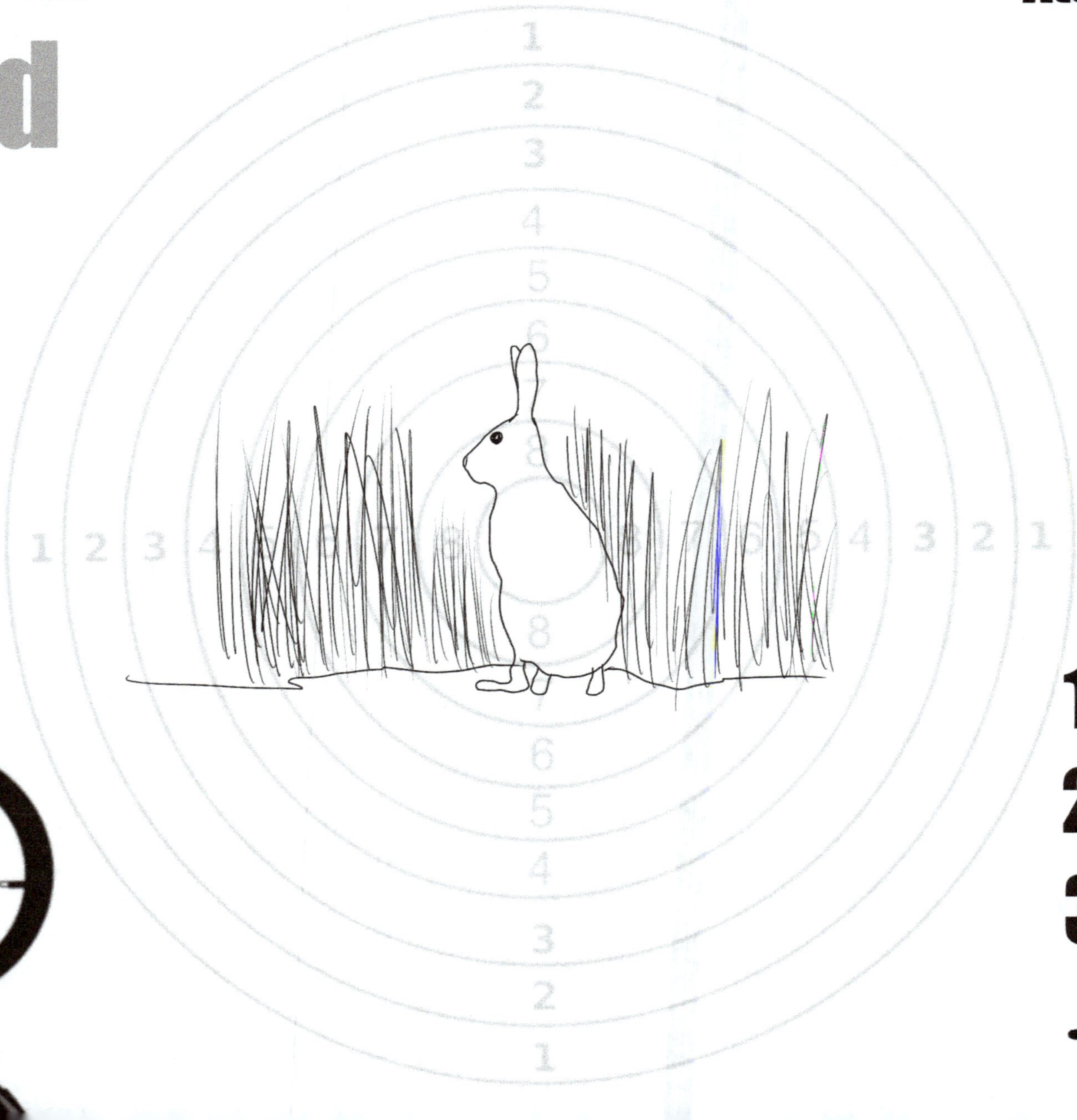

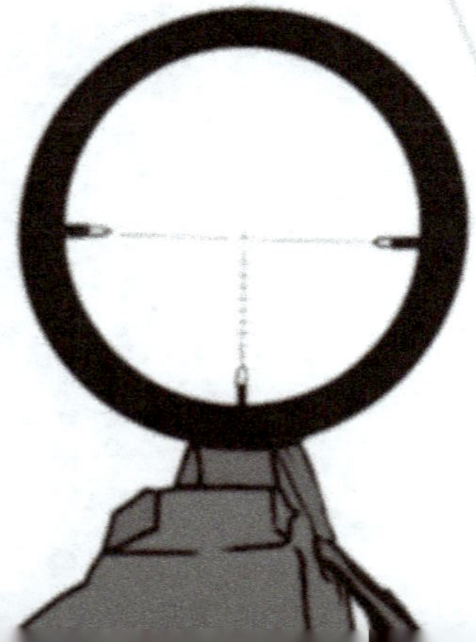

Points

1. ____

2. ____

3. ____

____

Difficulty level

Hard

Attempts

3

Points

1. ____

2. ____

3. ____

____

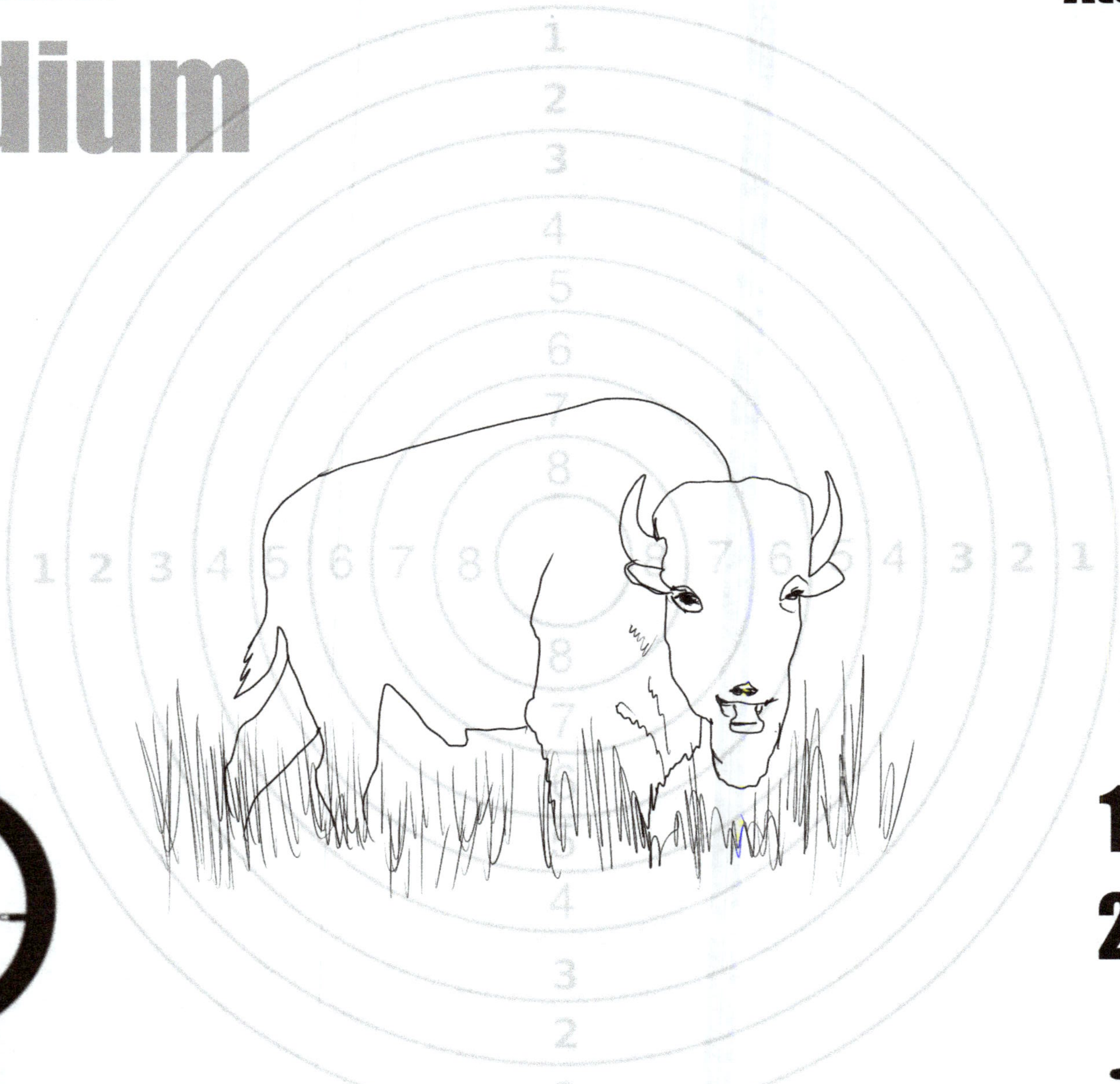

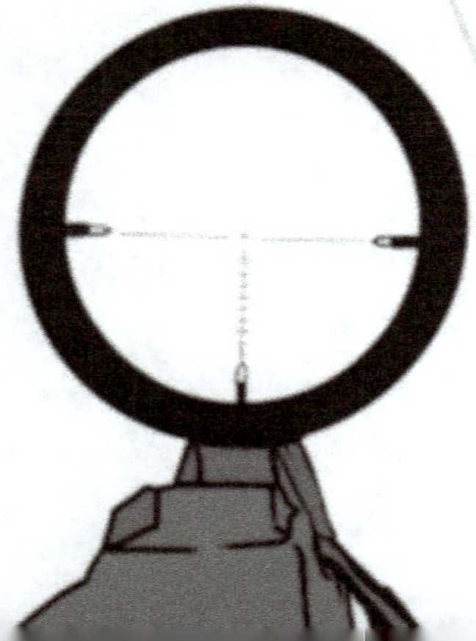

Points

1. ____

2. ____

____

Difficulty level
Easy
Attempts
1 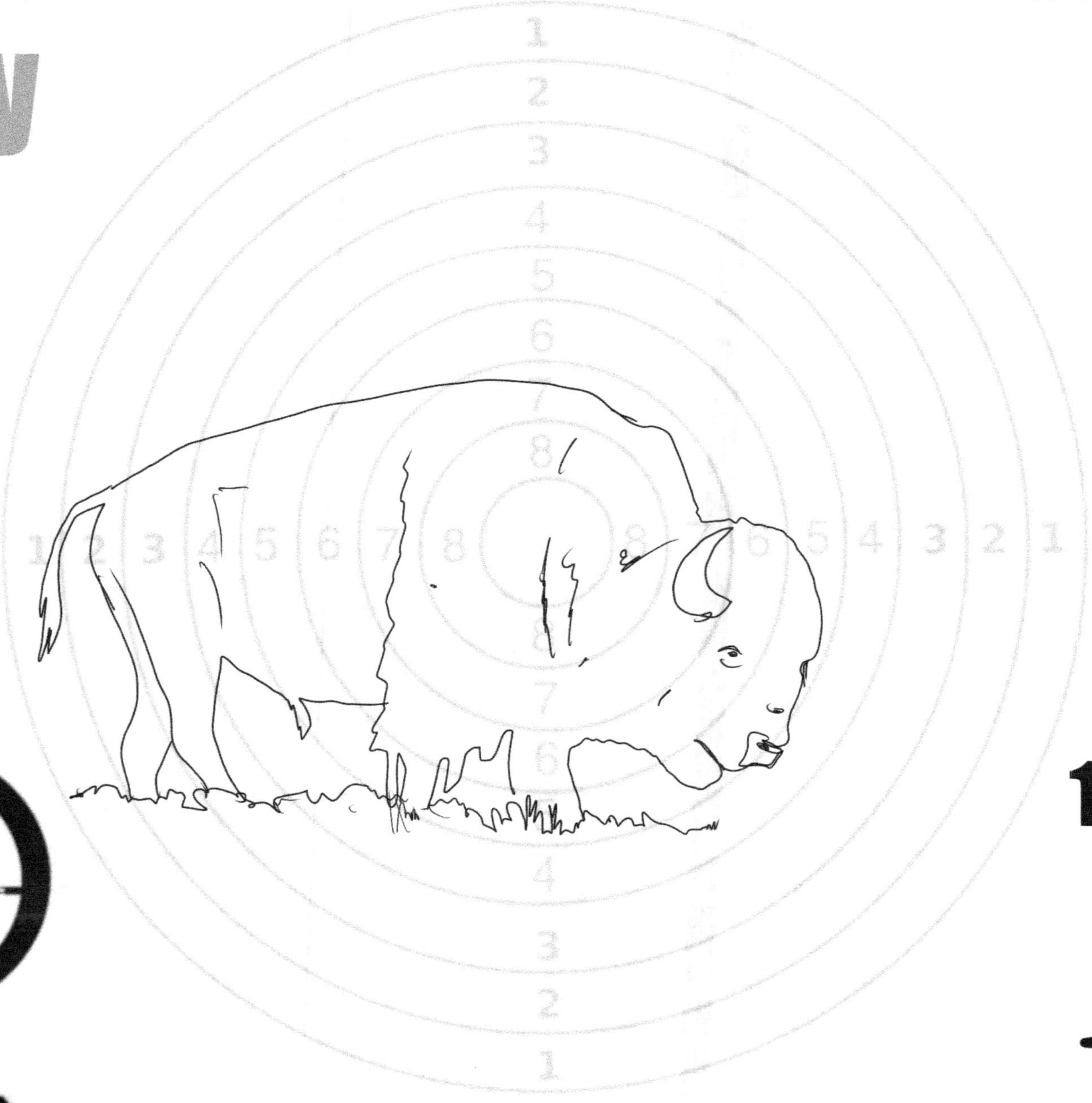 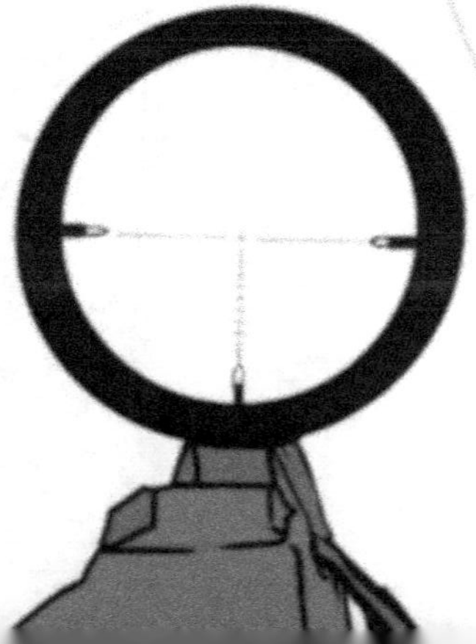
Points
1. ___

Difficulty level
Easy

Attempts
1

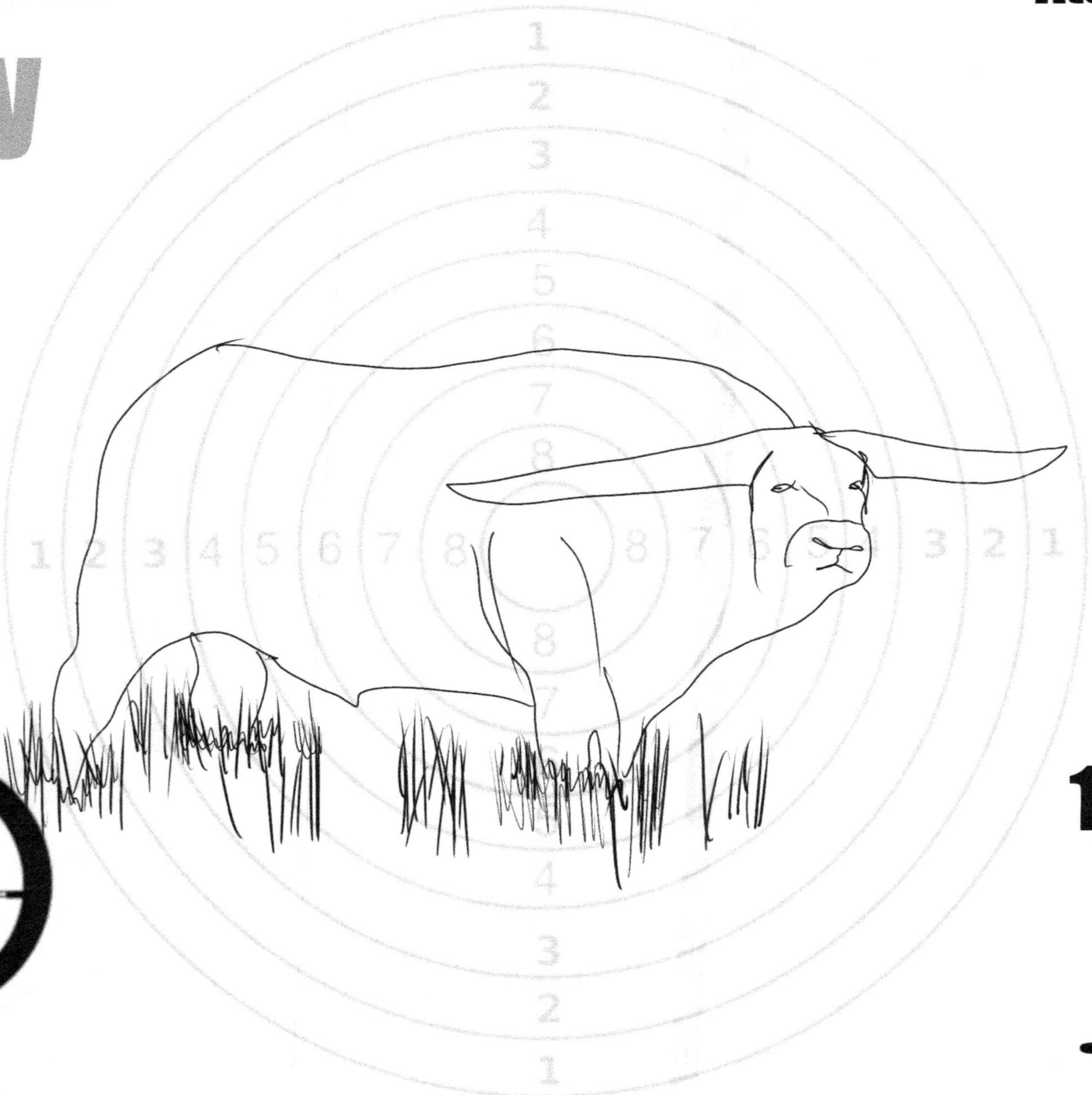

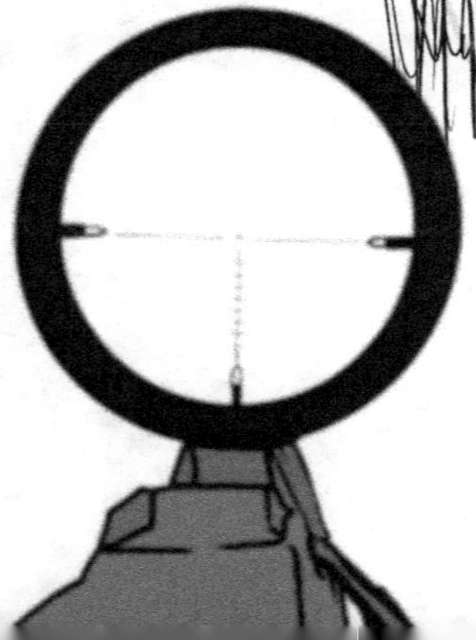

Points
1. ____

____

Difficulty level
Hard
Attempts
3  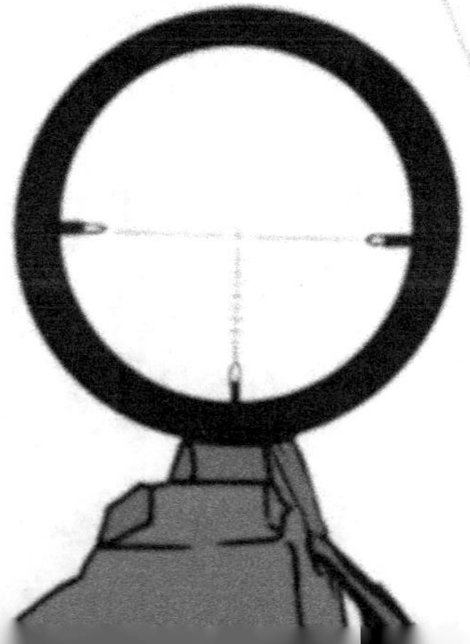
Points
1. ___
2. ___
3. ___

Difficulty level

Medium

Attempts

2

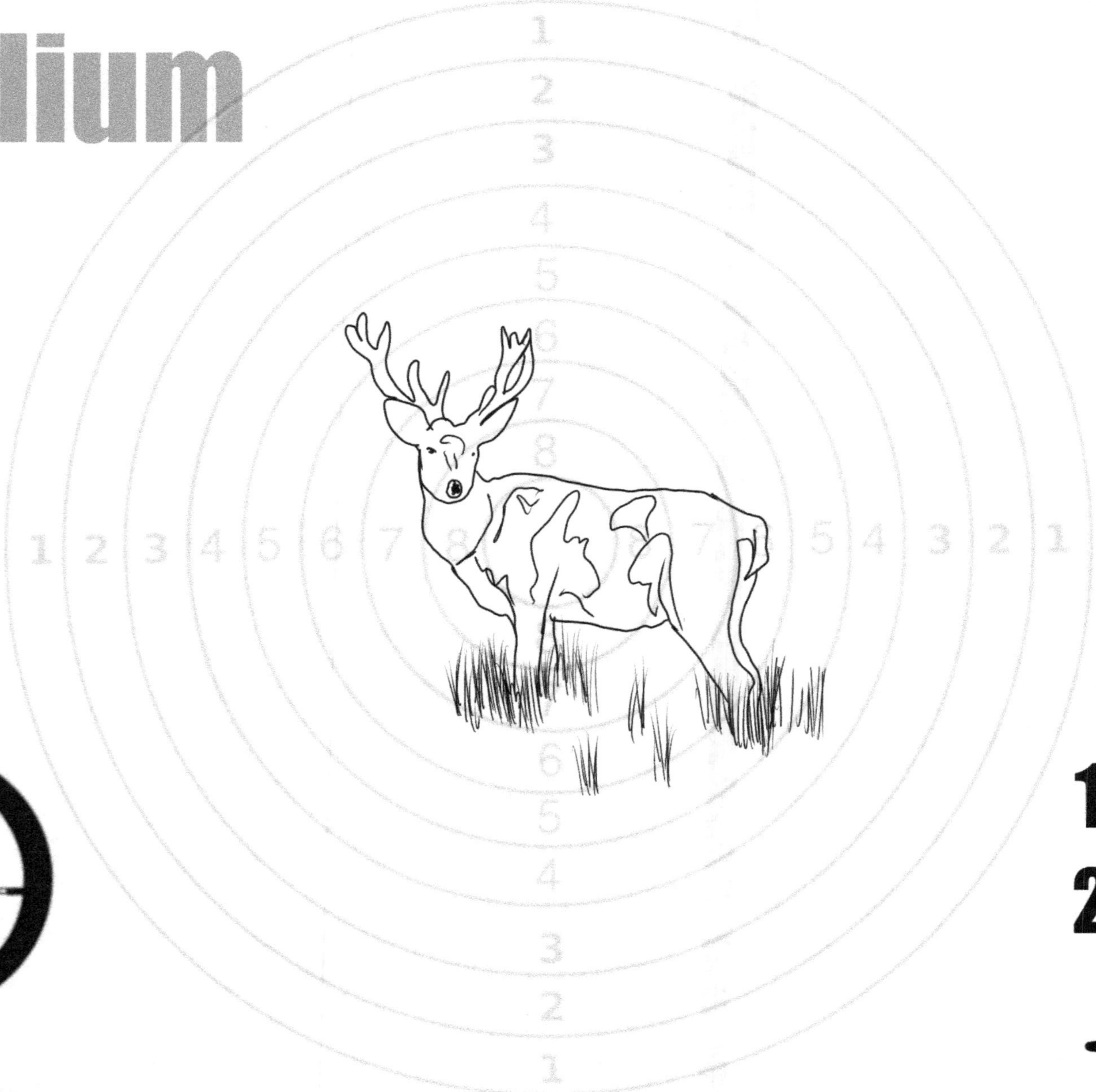

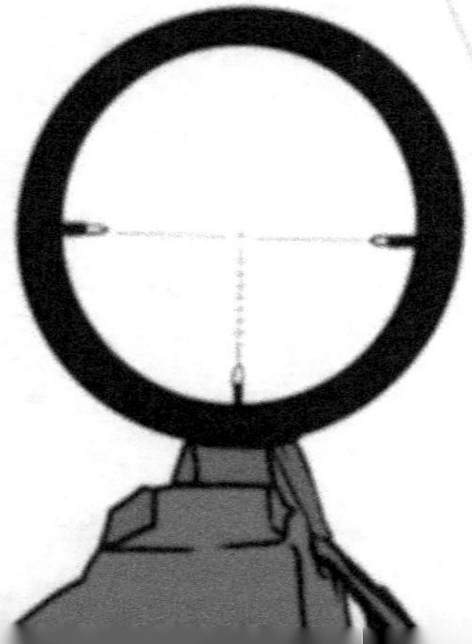

Points

1. ___
2. ___
___

Difficulty level
Medium
Attempts
2 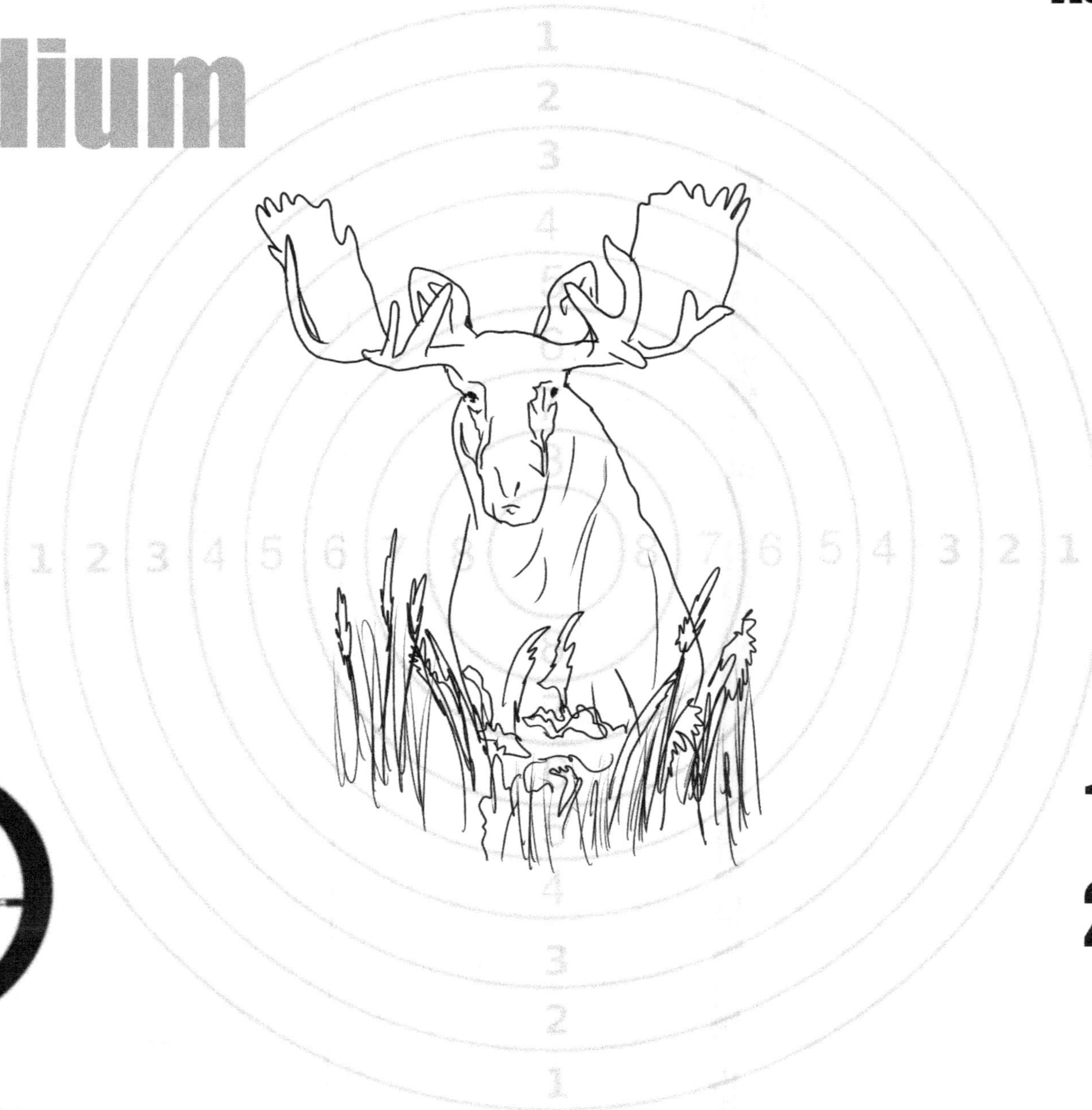 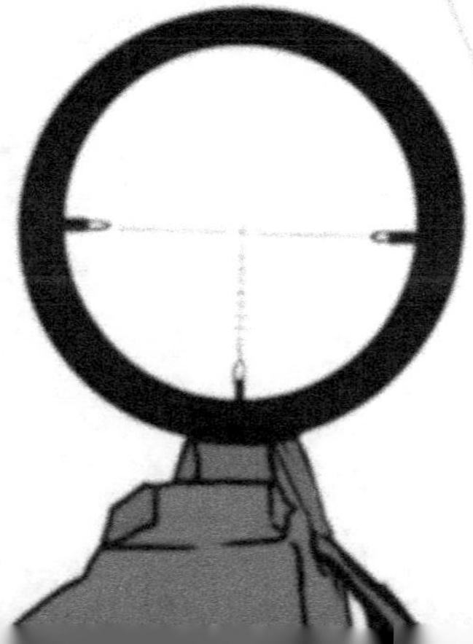
Points
1. ___
2. ___

Difficulty level
Medium

Attempts
2

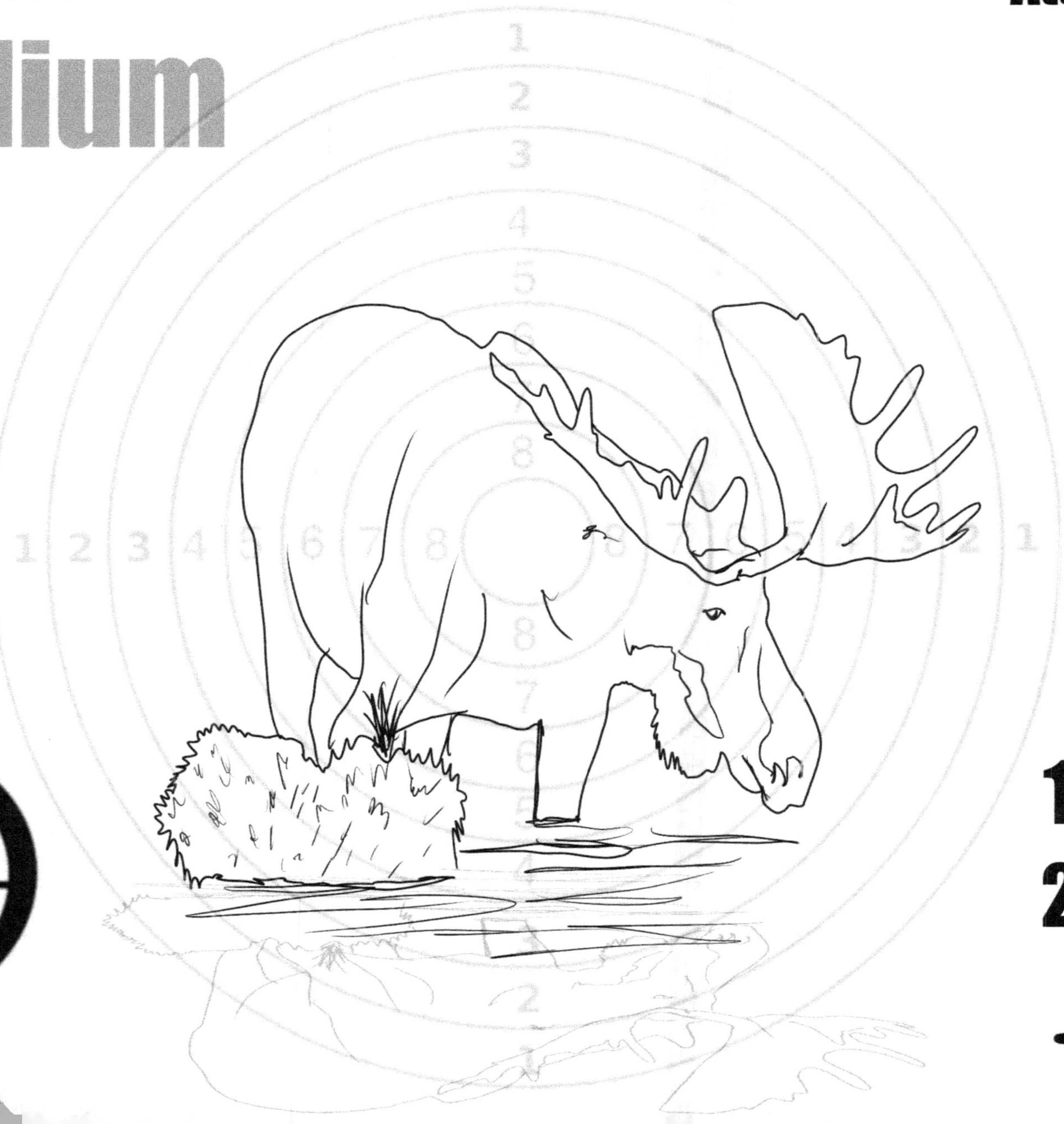

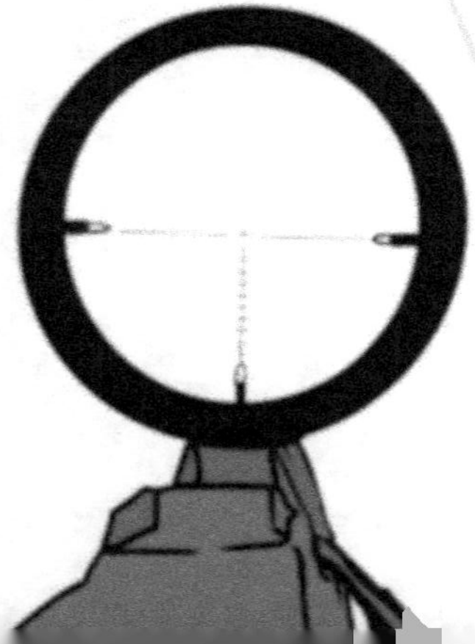

Points

1. ____
2. ____

____

Difficulty level
Easy
Attempts
1  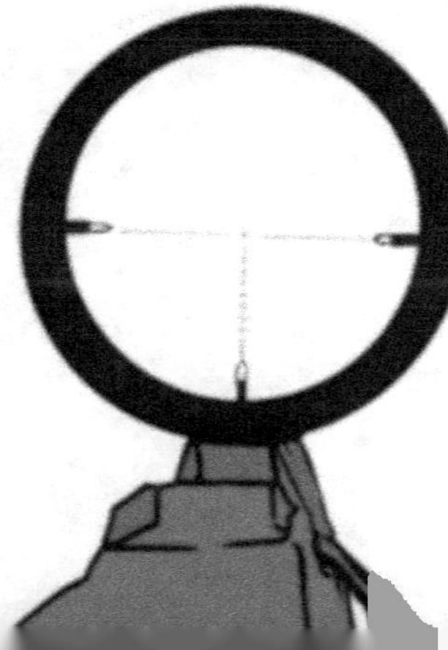
Points
1. ___

Difficulty level
Easy

Attempts

1

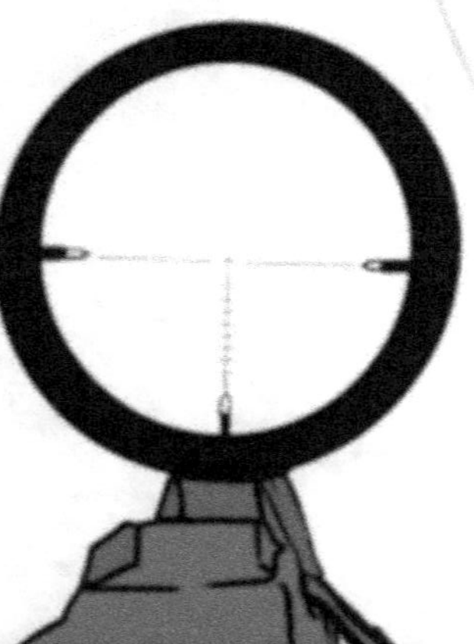

Points

1. _______

______

Difficulty level

Hard

Attempts

3

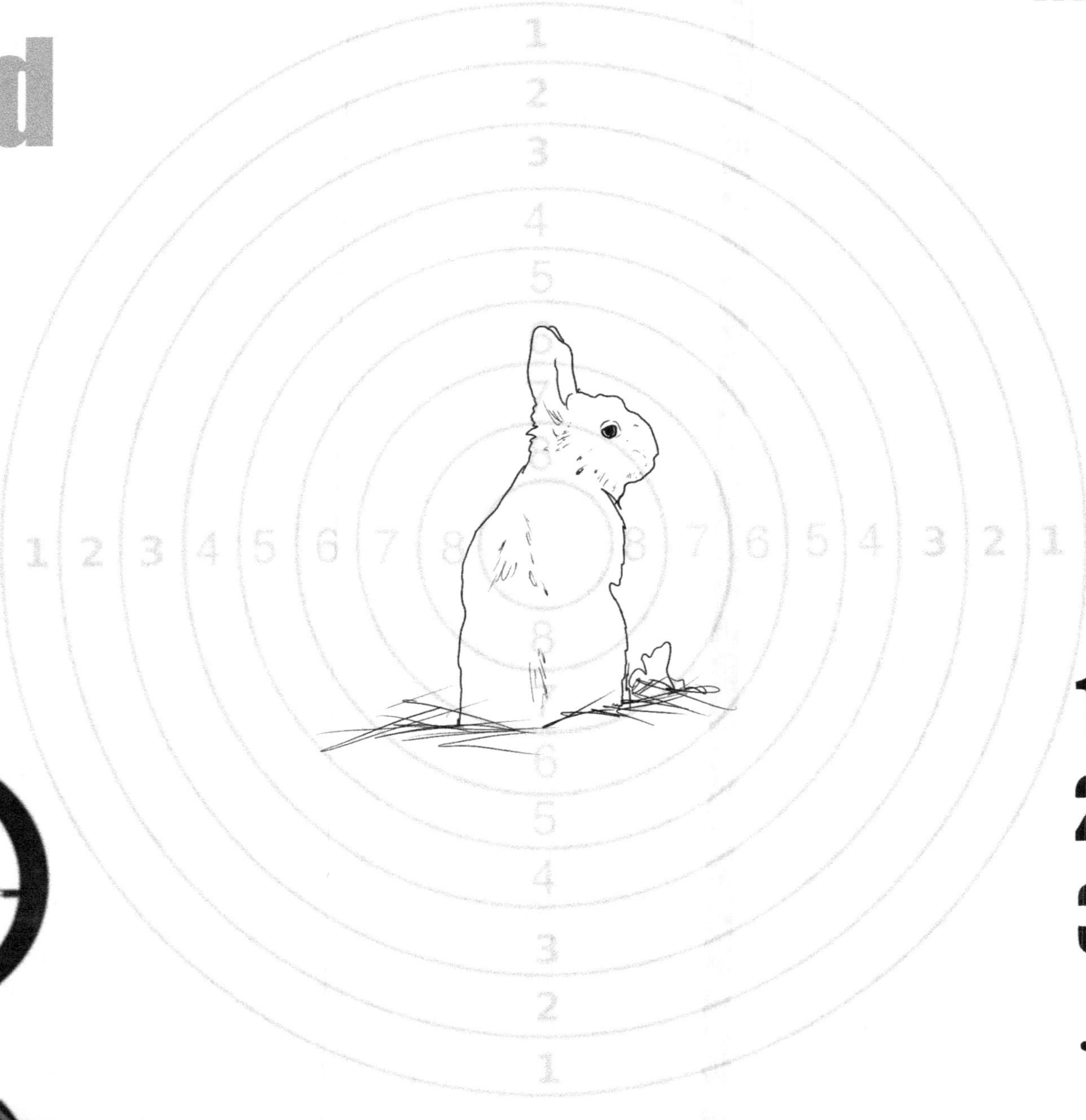

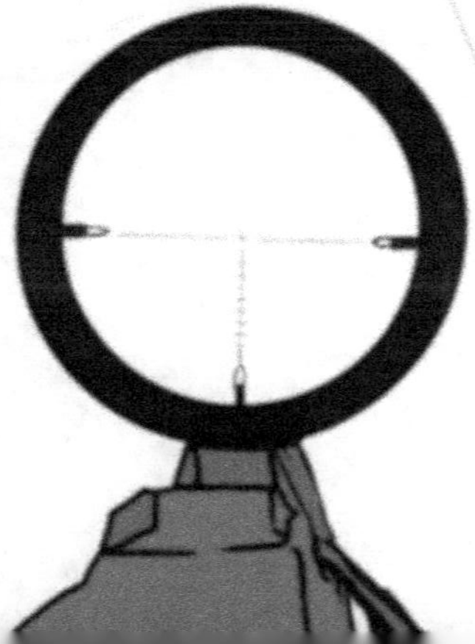

Points

1. ____

2. ____

3. ____

____

Difficulty level
Easy

Attempts

1

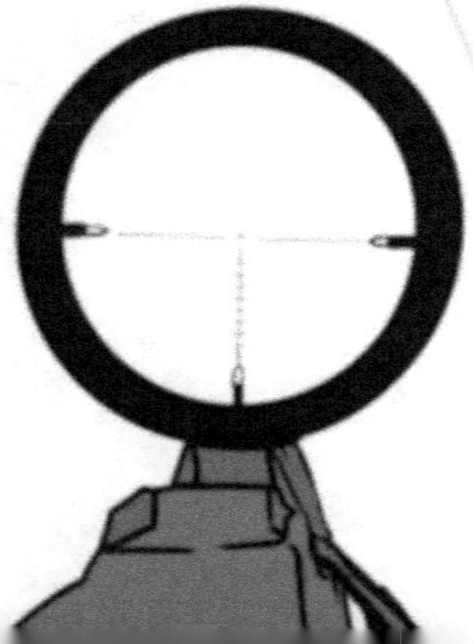

Points

1. ___

___

Difficulty level

Easy

Attempts

1

Points

1. ___

___

Difficulty level
Hard
Attempts
3 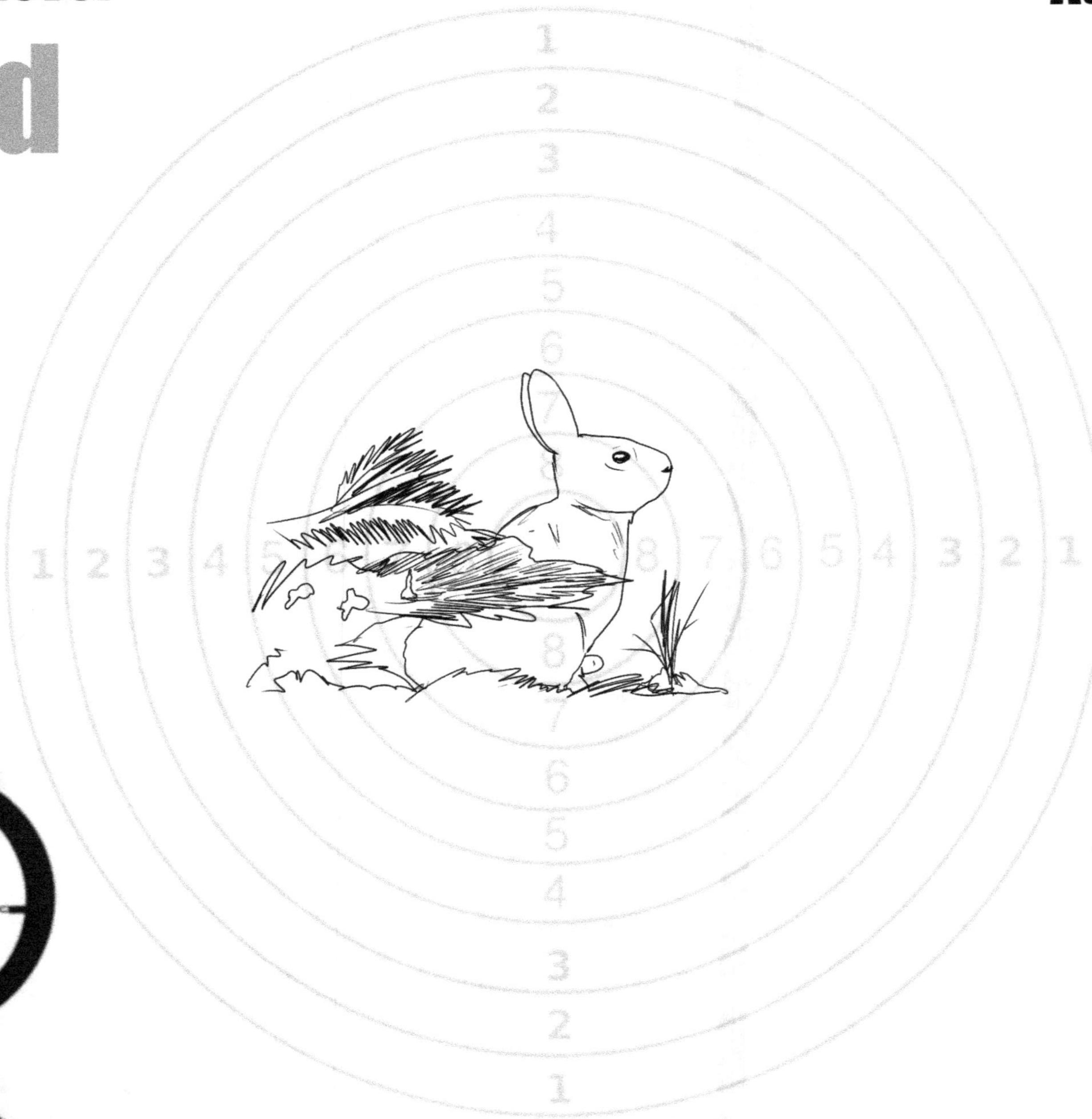 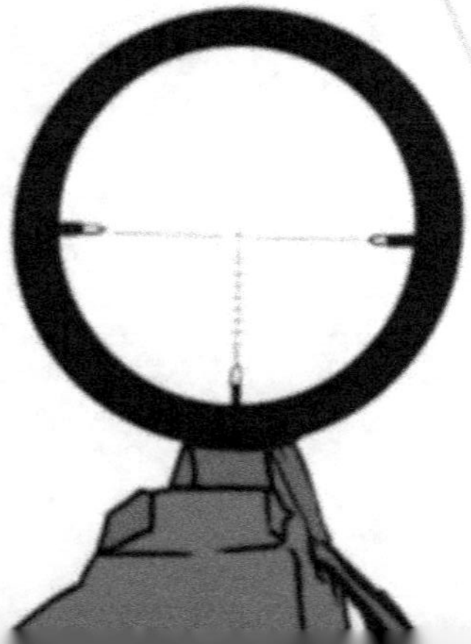
Points
1. ___
2. ___
3. ___

Medium

Points

1. ____

2. ____

1 2 3 4 5 6 7 8 8 7 6 5 4 3 2 1
1 2 3 4 5 6 7 8 8 7 6 5 4 3 2 1

Points

1. ____

____

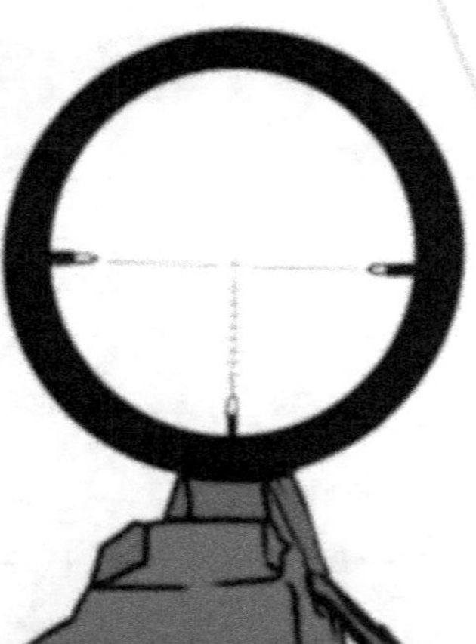

Difficulty level
Medium
Attempts
2
Points
1.
2.

Difficulty level
Hard

Attempts

3

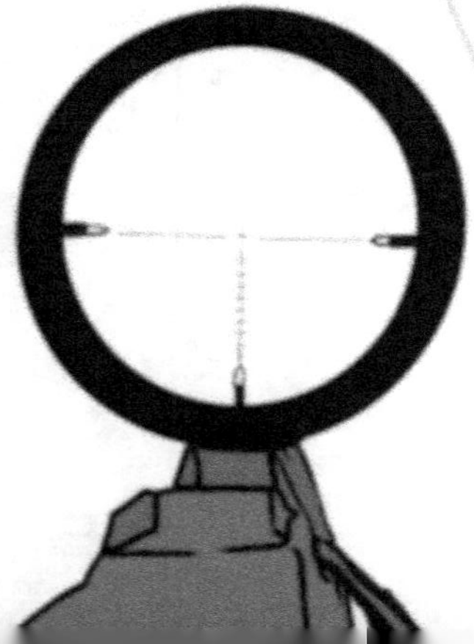

Points

1. ____
2. ____
3. ____

____

Difficulty level

Medium

Attempts

2

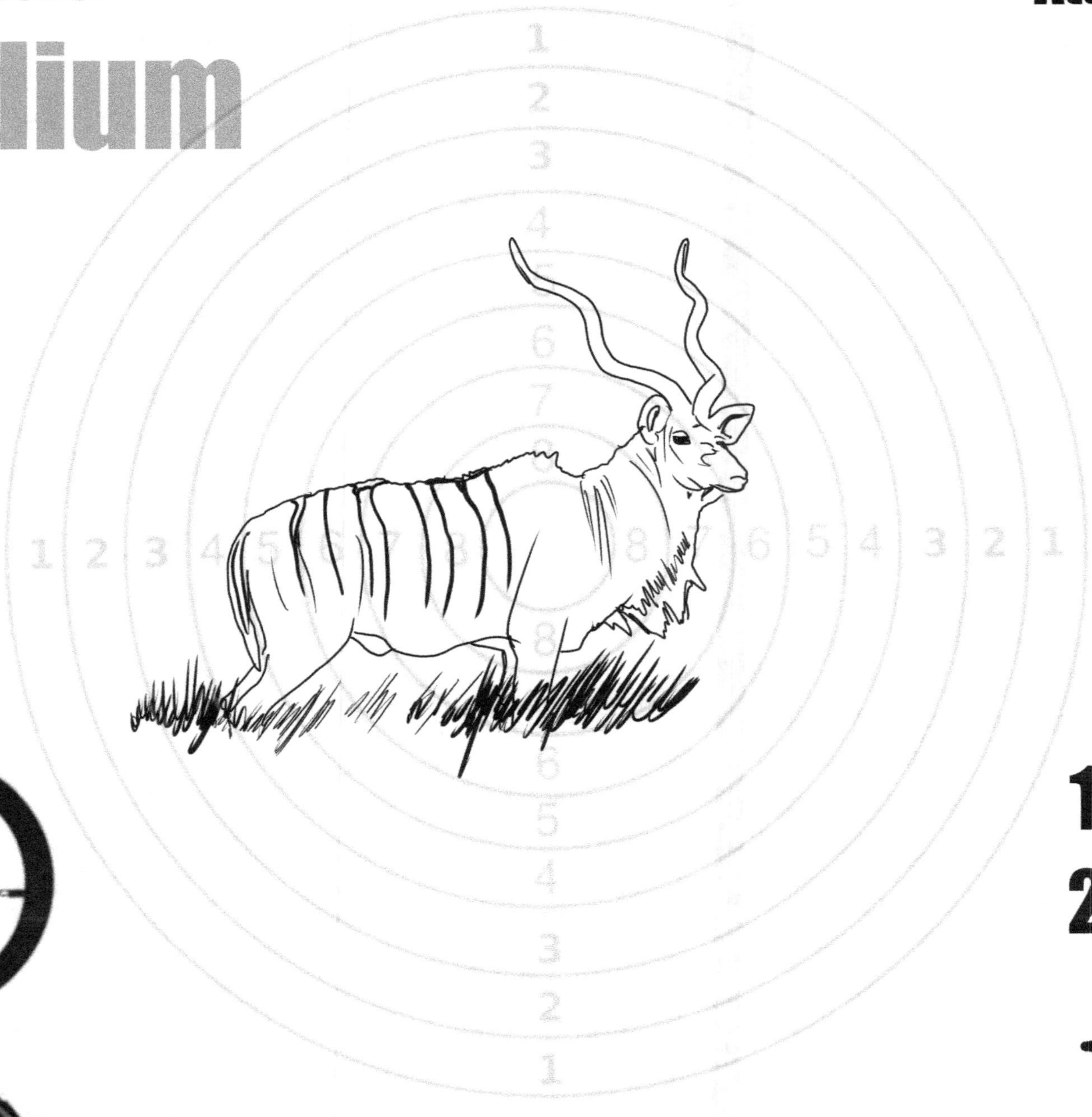

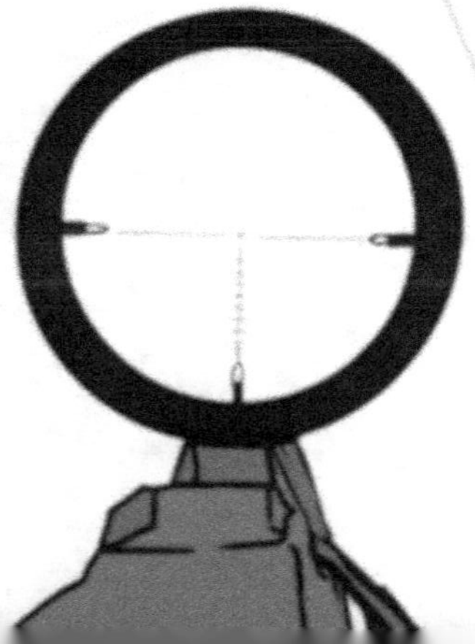

Points

1. ___

2. ___

___

Difficulty level
Medium

Attempts
2

Points

1. ___
2. ___
___

Difficulty level
Medium
Attempts
2  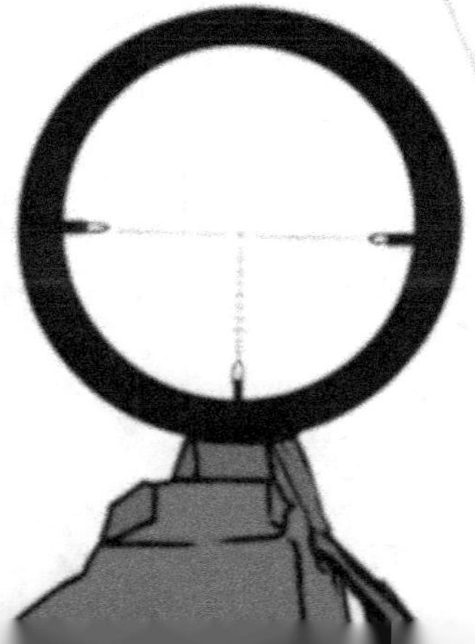
Points
1. ____
2. ____
____

Difficulty level

Hard

Attempts

3

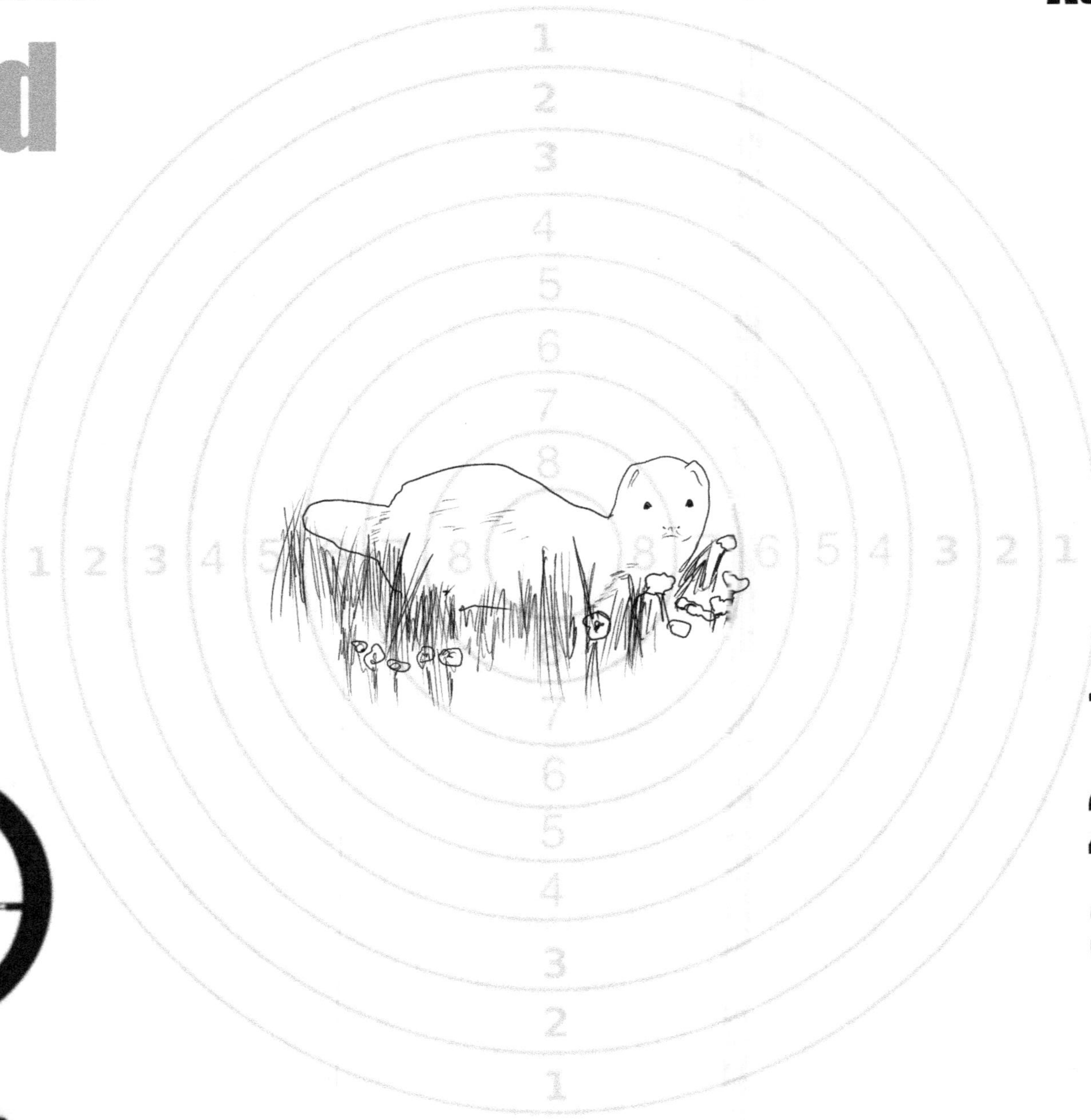

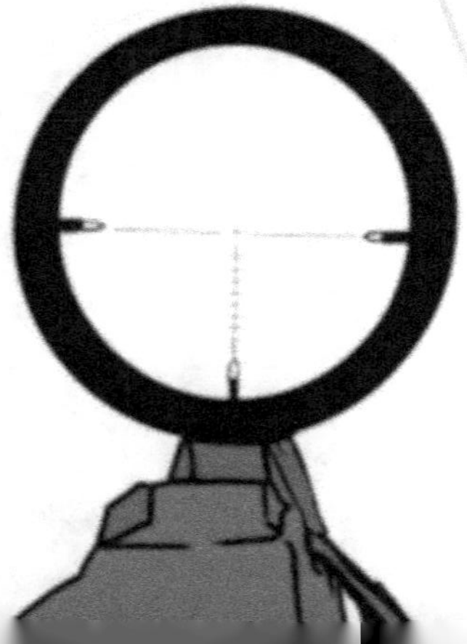

Points

1. ____

2. ____

3. ____

____

Difficulty level
Hard
Attempts
3
Points
1. ___
2. ___
3. ___

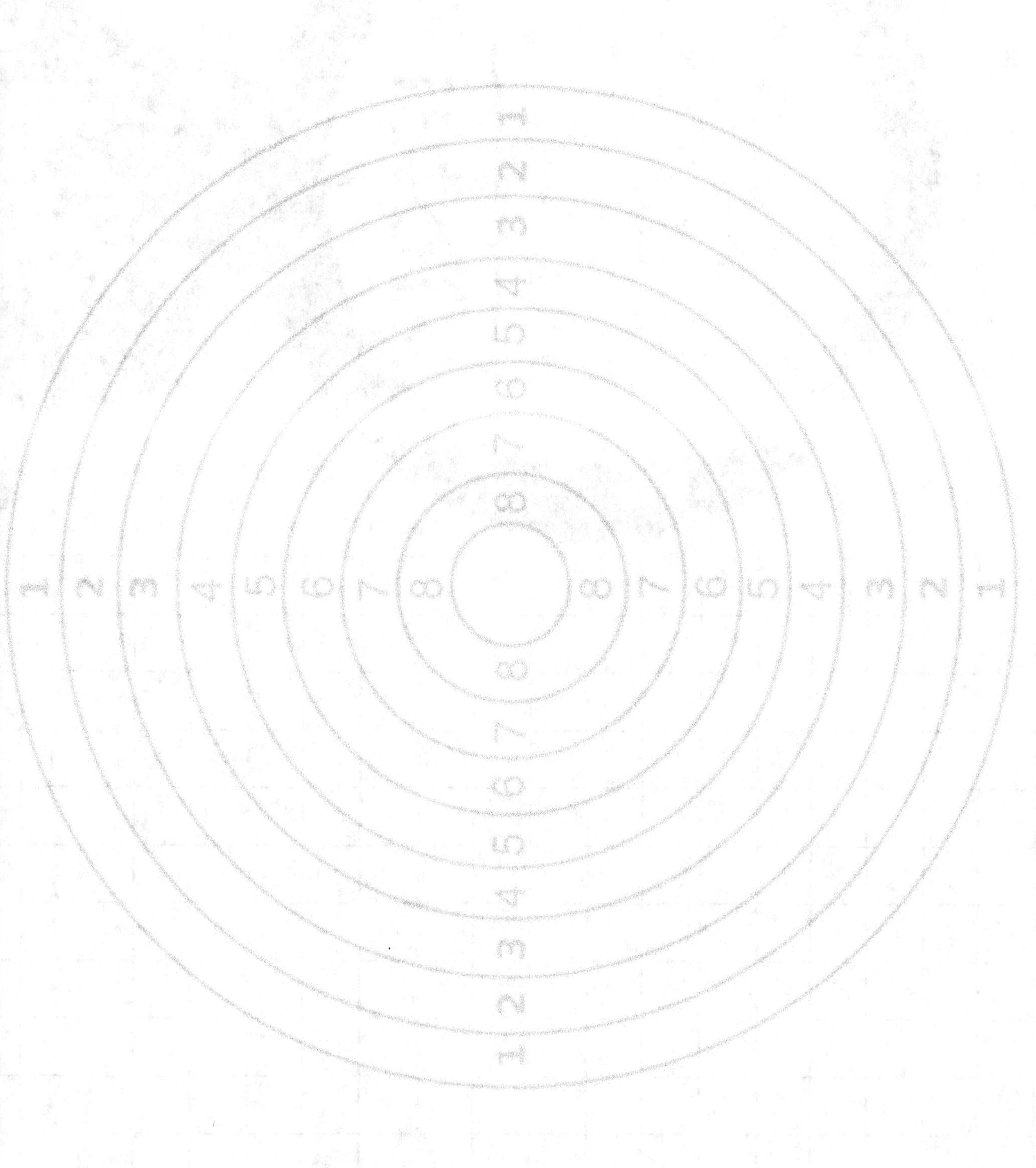

Add up your scores here

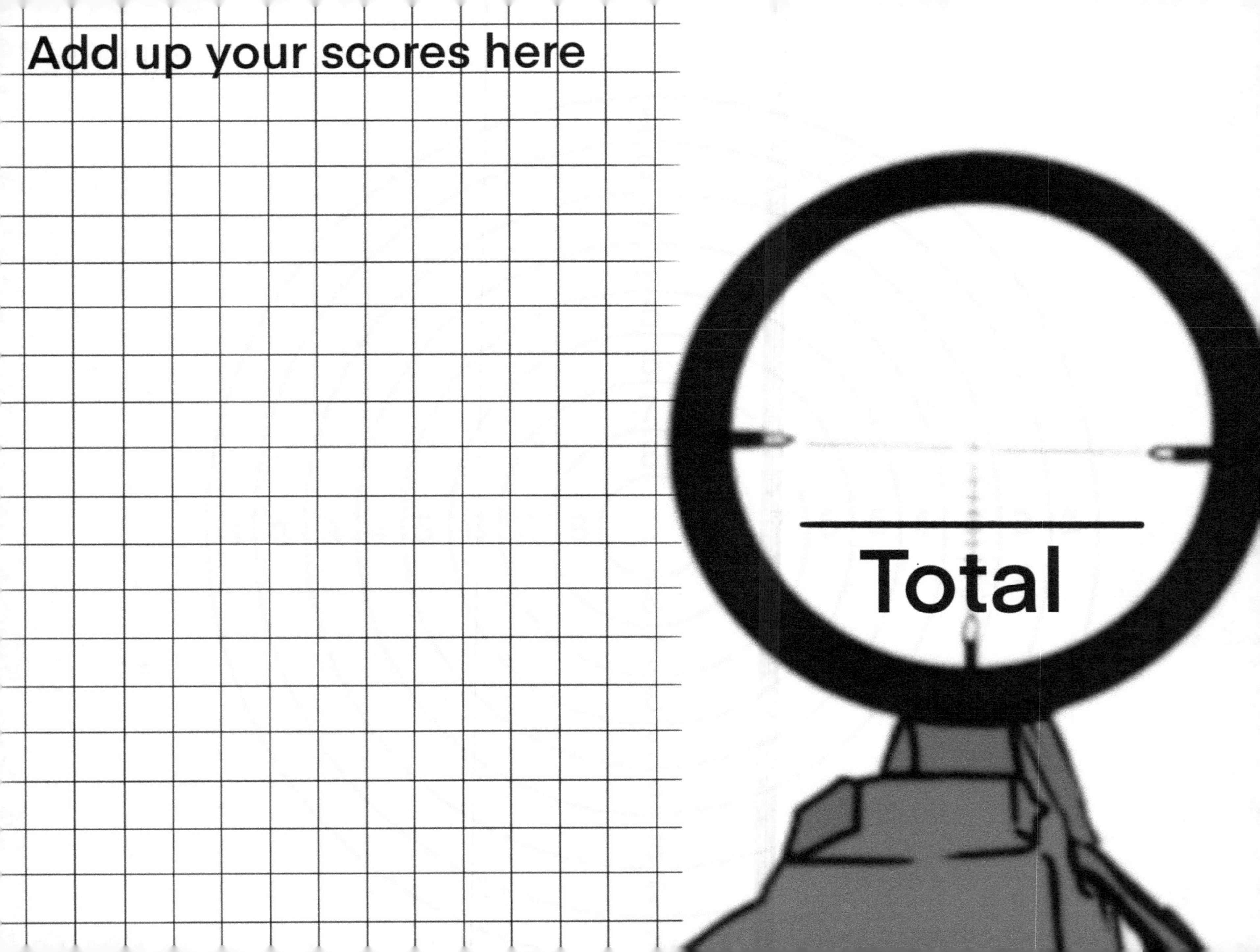

SCORES & TROPHIES

scores   **Award**

750-864
Expert

600-749
Intermediate

0-559
Rookie